Guide to the Christian Faith

An Introduction to Christia

by William A.

Here is a guide for t   no
wants to know what Ch.   bout,
and who wants a clue to   ng of its
great doctrines. Mr. Spurrier s   s why Christians believe what they do, what proofs exist to support them in their faith, and why some beliefs can be so relevant and powerful in meeting the problems of everyday life.

Mr. Spurrier's theme is that "belief determines action," and by belief he means basic convictions about important aspects of living —what one believes about his place in life, about evil, suffering, God, Christ, values, sin, faith and so forth. Only with mature knowledge of such topics can an adequate philosophy of life be realized in the complex world of today.

This is not a "theological" book written for the technically trained; it developed out of the author's actual experience with young people of college age. It may be considered a companion volume to the author's previous book, *Power for Action,* for *Guide to the Christian Faith* does for Christian doctrine what *Power for Action* did for Christian ethics.

GUIDE TO THE

CHRISTIAN FAITH

ALSO BY WILLIAM A. SPURRIER

POWER FOR ACTION:

AN INTRODUCTION TO
CHRISTIAN ETHICS

GUIDE TO THE
CHRISTIAN
FAITH

*AN INTRODUCTION
TO CHRISTIAN DOCTRINE*

BY

WILLIAM A. SPURRIER

1952

CHARLES SCRIBNER'S SONS, NEW YORK
CHARLES SCRIBNER'S SONS, LTD., LONDON

To
H. E. S.

PREFACE

THIS book is intended to help fill a gap. In the opinion of many clergy and laymen there is a wide gap between "theological books" and "popular religious books." Theologians tend to write for other theologians with the result that very scholarly and profound manuscripts are understood by only a few other learned men. The wisdom of the giants, therefore, is lost to the vast majority of people. On the other hand, the "popular religious books" are often merely self-help "potboilers," warmed-over sermons of optimistic encouragement, or thumbnail comments on the passing scene. Both types of books have their place and their value. But meanwhile, in an age of conflicting faiths—religious and secular—a vast number of people would like "to know what Christianity is all about." Some search diligently for the knowledge but are rebuffed by the scant information which is both available and readable. What seems to be needed is "middle-ground" information about the Christian faith. While the author hopes to provide a worthy contribution to the present need, he wishes to make it clear that he lays no claim to providing *the* complete, final, and authoritative filler. His hope is that this book may offer some guidance, some clue as to the meaning of the Christian doctrines.

The plan of the book is to describe *what* the doctrines are, *what* they *mean,* and *why* they make sense to Christians. Thus, some attempt is made to show *why* Christians believe what they do, why there does seem to be some "proof" of the validity of the historic doctrines, and why these doctrines can be so relevant and powerful in one's life. This is a large order and again the limitations of both the book and the author must be stressed. The book is only an introduction to Christian doctrine; the advanced reader may well find this "old stuff," and the interested may wish to dig deeper. Hence the suggested bibliography at the end. Further, it is hoped that this book will be but one of many similar ones in order that different viewpoints and presentations will help fill the "middle-ground gap."

A word should be said about the point of view of the author. This is not an "objective" book in the sense that it was written by an outsider impartially surveying Christianity. This is not a detached description of "what those Christians believe," as if the writer were not a Church member and didn't really care what Christians believe. The book is therefore obviously a "pro-Christian book." For the author is an ordained clergyman, professor of Christian ethics and Christian doctrine, and a firm believer in the Christian faith. On the other hand, it is to be hoped that this background does not inevitably mean that the presentation is narrow, bigoted, and uncritical. It is difficult to see how any professor could be unaware of the rigorous criticisms a college community—students and faculty alike—can make concerning the Christian faith. This is said with no bitterness but, rather, with gratitude. For unless one's religion can withstand the "slings and arrows" of genuine challenge, it is of little worth. Moreover, one learns so much from others, both about himself and the nature of life, that he is eternally grateful for such a fellowship of learning and experience. And if the writer understands the New Testament correctly, our faith *needs* the knowledge of other disciplines. Thus, it is hoped that the broadening background of the author will be apparent in the book.

As to theological labels which might be applied to the writer, it is difficult for him to choose the appropriate one. The word "broadening" above is a healthy adjective to some, but to others it is a sign of weakness. The author likes to think that the theological viewpoint in this book is in accord with the traditional orthodox Christian position. That is to say, the writer believes sincerely that the *essence* of what is said here is in harmony with the central beliefs of the majority of Christians throughout the Church's history. The *way* it is said is, perhaps, modern in that contemporary words, concepts, analogies are used. The details and applications may also be "liberal." It is the author's conviction, however, that what he *means* by "experiencing the God we know in Christ," is the same as what the majority of other Christians *mean,* whether in the first century, the fifth, sixteenth, or twentieth. The writer's *way* of describing it may be different, but he trusts the content of the doctrines, the truth behind the words are the same. To be quite personal on this problem, I would say that my way of describing this truth may not be the *best* way nor the most *accurate.* It is only one man's description and understanding, and therefore is seriously limited. For this reason, I earnestly hope that no one will regard this book as *the* definitive statement of *the* Christian faith. It would be a tragedy if some reader disagreed with some statement in this book and then felt that since he could not agree he could not be a Christian. My description is the most meaningful and clearest to *me,* but it may not be to someone else. Because I believe in the objective validity of experiences of God and man's ability to communicate to man, I believe that most descriptions and explanations can be understood and meaningful. Thus, in practice any book such as this will offer some help, some guidance. It would be terribly dull if everyone agreed with everything! As it is, one reader may find one part clear, another obscure and confusing. A second reader may find just the reverse—and so on. All that matters is that some people find some help here to either a beginning or further adventure in the Christian faith.

WILLIAM A. SPURRIER

ACKNOWLEDGMENTS

Before going on, I should like to acknowledge my indebtedness to the students and faculty of Wesleyan University because of their exceedingly friendly and rigorous sharing of criticisms which has enriched my life. Secondly, I am very much indebted to my secretary, Miss Kathleen Gratrix, who not only has to put up with me daily, but also cheerfully has had to decipher my hieroglyphics and laboriously type this manuscript. I am especially grateful to Professor Thomas Henney of the English Department, Wesleyan University, who kindly consented to do the tedious job of correcting my numerous mistakes in grammar. If any such mistakes still remain, it is entirely my fault; there is a limit to the number of corrections any man can make. Lastly, I am always indebted to my wife because of her constant encouragement and creative criticisms without which such work would become both a drudgery and a bore. Perhaps it should be added that the frequent interruptions of my two small sons provided "a touch of reality" that theology often either overlooks or obscures!

WILLIAM A. SPURRIER

May, 1951
Wesleyan University
Middletown, Connecticut

CONTENTS

GUIDE TO THE

CHRISTIAN FAITH

1

THE BELIEFS AND PURPOSE OF THEOLOGY

A. *Some Problems of Theological Writing*

THE purpose of this book is to describe as clearly and simply as possible the central Christian doctrines. This aim raises two problems for any author. First is the question of "what are the central doctrines?" This writer decided the question by noting which doctrines, throughout Christian history, received the most attention in the writings and creeds of the Church. The dogmas described in this book stand clearly in the historic tradition of the Church. However, it is also obvious that some other doctrines, such as those of the Virgin Birth, the Church, and the Apostolic Succession, while present in Christian theology, are not included in this book. The reason for these omissions is a personal decision of this writer. This decision rests on the conviction that the omitted doctrines are of secondary importance, and are derived from the primary doctrines which are contained in this book. Further, the author believes that such doctrines as the Church and the Virgin Birth cannot be understood adequately without a detailed and difficult examination of much technical scholarship. Such description, in the author's opinion, is out of place in this type of book. Lastly, the author recognizes the fact that other writers might not agree on the decision concerning the secondary doctrines. Many theologians, for example, might insist that the Doctrine of the Church is a primary tenet in the Christian faith. This writer might be will-

1

ing to agree, but would insist that he could not do justice to such a doctrine within the limits of this book. The author would point out, also, that the necessity of the Church is implied in many instances throughout the book, but adequate treatment cannot be supplied without doubling the length of the book.

The second problem is whether all the doctrines described here are of equal importance. To this question, the author must confess considerable ignorance. If by the phrase "equal importance" one means importance to the Christian faith, the answer would be that Chapters III through XII are of equal significance. If the phrase is taken to mean importance to the reader, this writer could not presume to answer with certainty. Chapter II, for example, was included because the author feels quite strongly that, for contemporaries, the problems of reason and faith, science and religion, must be discussed. In an earlier age, such topics would have been of minor relevance. Today, however, they constitute for many people a major barrier to the understanding of religion.

Again, the limitations of an introductory book such as this must be acknowledged. And the author would remind the professional scholar once more for whom this book is written. It is written for the average person who, regardless of age, is still young in mind and spirit. And the book is designed for all those who are at least partially attracted by Christianity, but who have some serious doubts as to just what the Christian faith stands for, and whether it is really relevant to daily living.

Unfortunately, "average persons" are perhaps a little bit frightened of the word "doctrine." Too often they imagine that doctrine and theology is a field in which only great theologians operate. The big words, the intricate arguments employed, may leave the average layman bewildered; and indeed he may wonder if such intellectual fireworks really matter anyway. We have all heard of the classic debate in the Middle Ages when theologians debated how many angels could stand on the head of a pin. Or, we may read of two religionists arguing even today about justification by faith and its relation to sanctification by the spirit—whatever that may mean. So, many may have felt that doctrine is something reserved alone for the theological sophisticates.

This situation has not been helped very much by the Church. Most theologians write only for other theologians, and most laymen or ministers write for Sunday school children. Very little has been written for the majority of adults in and outside the Church, although recently this lack has been recognized and a few books written for this specific need. (See Bibliography.) And it is hard to see how any of us can grow into the Christian faith if we don't know what it stands for. No intelligent modern will be satisfied with a religion that gives him an occasional "nice feeling," nor will he be attracted by a religious statement that "God is the unconditioned essence which is the ground of existence." What most of us desperately want and need is a definite set of beliefs about God, man, values, the meaning of life, and history. We want to know where we stand, and whether Christianity has anything to offer us in these turbulent times. We know that "good feelings," vague and pious hopes, and the seemingly archaic and ancient creeds are not enough. We want clear and understandable statements before we "sign up."

This book is an attempt to describe the basic Christian beliefs in language we can understand. And yet it should be obvious that such an attempt has many limitations. First, though all of us may want simple answers, life is far too complex to be described by grade school rhymes. And Christianity definitely rejects the notion that any mature religion can be summed up in some slogan—even the Golden Rule.

As we shall see later, the Rule may be Golden, but it could hardly be the sum total of either Judaism or Christianity. Second, in trying to explain Christian doctrines lucidly and clearly, there is always the danger of over-simplifying them and thereby falsifying them. Whether this is the case, the author can never be sure. Third, the book is by no means complete. It is really only an Introduction to Christian Doctrine dealing with the most central Christian beliefs and omitting consideration of many derived doctrines. Again, the beliefs are not treated historically. That is, no attempt is made to describe how each belief began and how it was changed and modified and argued about by various men down through history. Rather, the endeavor here is to describe what the basic beliefs of Christianity have been and are, in spite of the differences. What is attempted here is a restatement of those traditional Christian doctrines that have endured throughout the many squabbles and disagreements. Lastly, no absolute claim to truth can be made by the author. One cannot say that *he* presents *the* Christian faith without distortion or error. Some error, of course, is inevitable. The author is a Protestant and an Episcopalian and is, therefore, partially conditioned by these factors among others. But the problem would not be solved if he were an English Congregationalist or an Italian Catholic. We all live in different environments with different influences. On the other hand, some claim can be made to presenting the Christian faith at least partly correct because each of us received his knowledge of Christianity through the Church, that is to say, the Bible, Church history, theologians, creeds, other Christian people. Which parts of the book are "true" and which are in error, the author cannot say. If he could, he would cut out the errors, obviously. All he knows and hopes is that there is enough of basic Christianity to appeal to the readers, help them to understand the Christian faith more clearly and perhaps to be a guide to further study and, better still, further Christian living.

B. *The Importance of Beliefs*

A common attitude today is the idea that "actions speak louder than words," that "what you believe doesn't matter; it's what you do that counts." Americans especially have a great impatience with ideas and thoughts and theories. We say "we want action" and that "we'll talk about it afterwards." We call constantly for the "practical man" and suspect the theorist will only confuse and mislead us, and what is worst of all, will never get anything done. This attitude apparently does not consider whether forthright actions may lead us into trouble or not, or whether practical activity may not be quite impractical later on. The assumption seems to be that so long as people are rushing around doing things, somehow everything will turn out all right. And often when it appears that such activity is not solving problems, we get even more impatient and demand even more intense activity. Perhaps it is time to stop and find out if we are really going anywhere or just going around in circles.

This same attitude is carried over into the field of religion. Many religious folk say that what you believe about religion doesn't matter, it's what you do. "Never mind all the prattle about creeds and doctrines, be a good neighbor, that's what counts." And we can always find somebody in the Church who knows a lot of doctrine and theology, but whose morals leave something to be desired. When we find one of these we stop and say, "See what I mean?" Of course, actions are important and they do speak louder than words. Knowledge can never be a substitute for responsible action. What we do is terribly important. But what we have forgotten is that what we do is dependent upon what we believe. *Belief determines action*. This is such an obvious psychological and religious truth that one might think it hardly needed explaining, but perhaps it is so obvious that we have neglected it.

Belief determines action, but what are beliefs? They should be distinguished from opinions. Opinions are various notions about all kinds of subjects, such as baseball, movies, guesses about the weather, the elections, general ideas about the political situation, or general economic worries. Opinions are not idle fancies, nor are they strong prejudices. Opinions are the stuff of most of our small and not so small talk. Beliefs, on the other hand, as used in this book, mean our basic convictions about important problems. Beliefs deal with meanings of life, the important aspects of living—what do I believe about my place in life, about evil and suffering, tyranny, God, values, fellow man? A belief, therefore, implies not only a strong conviction about something, but a reliance, a trust in what you believe. Thus, a man may believe that his neighbors are basically selfish and "out to get him." If he really believes that, trusts it, he will react in very definite ways. This belief will direct much of his activity. Either he will move out of the neighborhood, or, if he can't do that, he will probably build a wall around his house, have a couple of dogs, take out burglar insurance, snub his neighbors, always suspect the worst of them, isolate himself, and generally be a social misfit. Why? Because he has anti-social notions? That doesn't say anything. All it says is: Mr. X is anti-social because he does anti-social actions. That is the equivalent of saying an apple is an apple because it is an apple. The question about Mr. X should be, "Why is he anti-social?" And if we trace the cause back just a little, we would find that he is anti-social because of a belief about his fellow man. The belief may be unconscious in him. It is not the function of this book to discover how he got the belief. For our purposes, what is important is the belief and the fact that it determines what he does.

Everybody, then, has beliefs. The question is never the argument between, "Will you have some beliefs," or "Will you have no beliefs?" The only real question is, "Which set of beliefs do you live by and are they true?" So, at the outset, the Christian faith must reject the prevalent idea that beliefs don't matter. It seems obvious that they do matter and matter intensely, especially in these days even more so than perhaps thirty years ago. For there are many sets of beliefs now—political, economic and religious—which claim the devoted following of many millions of people. If one is a Communist he has a definite set of beliefs and these convictions lead him to a definite set of actions. If one is a pessimist about life, his actions will be very different from those of an optimist. A democrat believes certain things and so votes democratic; a republican believes other things, and so acts or votes differently. Beliefs don't matter? They literally make all the differences in the world! One might go almost as far as to say, "Tell me what a man's actions are, and I'll tell you what he believes." So, in the Christian religion beliefs are all-important because they will determine the person's actions. A man's conscious beliefs may be one thing and his unconscious beliefs or "reliances" another, in which case, his actions will frequently be dictated by his unconscious convictions. This is what usually happens in the case of a hypocrite. The problems of getting the two sets of beliefs together harmoniously is again not the purpose of this book. But I am very sure that even this problem can't be solved unless consciously we know what the Christian beliefs are in the first place!

C. *The Province of Theology*

The word theology, like doctrine, has also scared us. It need not. Theology is concerned with beliefs about God, the nature of life, and man's relationship to God and life. Thus, Christian theology is not some mysterious mumbo-jumbo. It is a system of beliefs, though not complete, put forth by great Christians about these problems. Theology is a description of what these men have experienced and thought about in a common enterprise—life with God.

But it is precisely the descriptions which bother people. Theology seems to be a mass of conflicting and confusing beliefs, rather than a unified, simple, and clear-cut system. The reason for the differences of belief is obvious. Nobody knows all the answers to all of life's problems; nobody can know all about God and the nature of reality; each person is different; each has different experiences. This seems to me not at all unusual. It would be shocking to me if there were complete agreement on all beliefs. Such agreement would indicate that there was no honesty anywhere in Christian history, or that all Christians were dumb slaves. The apparent disunity, then, is due to varied experiences in varying languages of various men in various cultures in various ages of history!

What is remarkable is that there is so much unity. For example, look at the Bible which covers some 2,000 years of history and is filled with all kinds of variances and opposing sets of beliefs. In spite of all its "disunity," the Bible is marked by singleness of theme and content. Throughout the whole collection the subject remains constant: the relationship of God and man and history, the progressive revelation to man of God through priests and prophets, and finally Jesus Christ. But more about this later. There is a rope of continuity and identity in Christian theology on which hang the other strands of differing beliefs.

If one is interested in discovering the unity and diversity of beliefs and in distinguishing between them, one can study the cultural and psychological background of each theologian and the times in which he lived. For no one lives in a vacuum; no one experiences "truth" or writes "pure thoughts" which have no relation to his surroundings and

critics. Christianity and its theologians have always had to
face cultural and religious challenges and each problem required different emphasis. The criticism of Christianity made
in one century had to be answered, but the challenges of another century were different and so required seemingly different answers. For example, during the first days of Christianity in Palestine, the Jews wanted to know why they should
accept Christianity. Hence, the Gospel of Matthew tries to
answer Judaism in terms the Jews could understand. That is
why Matthew is filled with Old Testament references. But a
short fifty years later, it was the Greeks who challenged
Christianity. Since the Greek criticism assumed a more philosophical background, Matthew was of little use here. The
Gospel of John, however, was written precisely for the Greek
mind, and therefore it is more philosophical in presentation
and has very few Old Testament references and concepts.
Obviously, there are marked differences between Matthew
and John. These authors were talking to different people and
answering different criticisms. But there is a unity and similarity in the two gospels. Both agree in the whole problem
of God's relation to man; both agree in the nature of Christ
and His centrality to the Christian faith. Matthew uses the
idea of Messiah in describing Christ as the revelation of God;
John uses the Greek word "Logos" to convey the same idea.
And so the process of cultural adoption continues through
history. Later, Christianity was challenged by Roman authors
with the great legal ideas—thus requiring answers that would
appeal to the legal and stoic mind. Later still, the Renais-
sance and Age of Enlightenment were serious challenges to
Christianity. These required still other types of answers. In
our own day, Christian thinkers must take the worship of
science into account. That is why this book begins with a
relatively long section on science, reason and faith. In other
ages, science was hardly a problem and could have been

handled in a footnote. Much of the apparent diversity within Christianity is not disunity or contradiction, but rather different ways of presenting the same basic ideas. Most of the bitter trouble and misunderstanding is due to ignorance. Too many people have taken some few beliefs and have taken them literally, without understanding how they came to be formulated and the meaning behind the words. If the real nature of theology is more clearly understood, much of the trouble could be avoided. As I shall try to make clear later on, theology is not static; it is not a rigid set of definitions; it is a dynamic process which operates on the same problems —primarily those concerning the relation of God to man. It is also constantly revising itself, criticizing itself both from within and without, continually seeking new and clearer explanations. Theology is thus a continuing process, a set of guideposts. It is never the last word, the complete encyclopedia about all of life.

For these reasons, it seems to me that doctrine, or theology, is one of the foundations of Christianity and the Church. The lack of doctrine or the lack of knowledge of beliefs is one of the main causes of Christian disunity. Within Protestantism itself there is virtually no disagreement on the central problems of theological beliefs, though there is a healthy disagreement on formulations. The main Christian doctrines are present in almost all the denominations. What keeps us apart are small secondary beliefs, such as the precise manner of ordination, or the amount of liturgy. Or, more often, one denomination *thinks* another denomination believes in the total depravity of man, when it really doesn't at all. And of course, there are always the psychological problems which separate us. Church A just doesn't like the people in Church B across the street. By and large, however, uneducated ministers and laymen who have no real knowledge of Christian doctrine are the chief barriers to the union of Protestantism.

For in place of solid Christian beliefs, these people have a host of cultural beliefs which they assume are the same as Christian beliefs and, indeed, label them as such. That is why today in America vast numbers of people identify Christianity with capitalism and democracy. There is much good in all three, but neither capitalism nor democracy can be fairly equated with Christianity, or vice versa. Also, the idea of freedom in America has come to mean virtually license. When applied to religion, many people say that freedom means the opportunity to believe whatever you want to believe, or freedom to believe nothing at all. Christianity does not include such a definition of freedom. There is plenty of freedom in Christianity, but not unbridled fancy of ideas. There has to be some common agreed-upon base from which to operate freely and tolerantly. Diversity and disagreement are both necessary and healthy, if they are contained within some agreed and unified area. For example, we are all Americans in the U.S.A.; therefore, we can differ on how to run our country. As Christians we have a common faith and set of experiences and beliefs about God; therefore, we can differ as to what these may mean precisely in all areas of life and action. But it is the spirit, the shared experiences and basic beliefs which unite us and enable us to act freely and creatively together—and to do so with respect, toleration, and affection.

One thing should be clear, the unity of Christendom will not occur while people believe nothing or anything they want to believe and while they suppose they can then act all alike. Unity will come only if doctrines are made clear and decisive and yet made to retain their dynamic guiding character. Let us look, then, at the basic Christian beliefs with the hope that at least a start may be made here towards understanding the nature of the Christian faith and its meaning for us in our daily lives.

2

REASON AND FAITH

A BOOK on Christian doctrine might logically begin with a statement of the Doctrine of God. But these days one cannot discuss God without risking at once serious argument about faith and reason. For many moderns an understanding of the nature, authority, and relevance of faith and reason is the greatest intellectual barrier to religion; it is essential, therefore, that a satisfactory solution be found to this problem. Many people still tend to define faith as "believing something that isn't so." Many other people associate faith with guesswork, with long-range hope, or with blind acceptance of some creed. Reason, on the other hand, they tend to regard as the only way to truth. A crude expression is the statement that "common sense" is the great test of anything. If something is not capable of clear rational proof, the verdict is that it should be abandoned. Just what common and horse sense is has never been made clear, but that seems to be the great slogan of truth.

Of course, reason has been under severe attack in the last fifty years. The violence, irrationality, and madness that have appeared in the most civilized and cultured countries in world history have shaken man's naive trust in the power of reason. And some schools of modern psychiatry have done much to show that reason does not control human behavior. Consequently, there has been a qualification of our trust in the power of reason to control our destinies. In some cases, the reaction has been so extensive as to suggest that reason cannot and should not guide human behavior. And this may be equally naive and dangerous.

Yet, even if many people are more suspicious of reason nowadays, some have only transferred their loyalty from reason to some part of science. Science alone seems to be the only avenue to truth. Thus today, many people still believe faith deals with things that can't be proved, with uncertain and probably unimportant matters; while science, on the other hand, is something you can trust. Perhaps it is not too far from the mark to say that science, for the average person, has replaced religion as the hope of man. Advertising, for example, usually underlines the word "scientific" in order to prove the value of a product. Many people carry this reverence for science over into their religion where the problem takes on new proportions. Most of the issues religion deals with can't be proved in the science laboratory. One can hardly find God in a test tube, nor see Christ under a microscope, nor discover the specific heat of love, nor the density of justice. These problems cannot be put into mathematical formulae nor even into logical syllogisms. Because religion cannot "prove" or "demonstrate" its beliefs and truths this way, most people thereby conclude that religion is false. For them, the scientific method is the sole test of truth. Not only are non-scientific answers to life's problems regarded with skeptical disdain, but the very fact that the problem cannot be reduced to a scientific statement may suggest to some that the problem itself doesn't exist. Thus, it is obvious that if this "scientific viewpoint" is right, religion is defeated at the start. A barrier has been set up that cannot be breached—unless we examine the barrier itself.

This discussion of science and religion is not new. To many mature intellectuals it must seem shopworn. This debate has been going on for over two hundred years and in the minds of most great thinkers has been settled; it is no longer a problem. It seems obvious to them that both religion and science are valid, that both are dealing with different aspects of life, and that both are indispensable. The fact remains, however, that most young people and a large majority of adults still believe that science and religion are in sharp conflict. This conflict is still a very real and prominent problem for them. And I suspect that even among the intellectuals it is still a problem, too. Few intelligent people today would care to argue on behalf of a narrow experimental science as over against all other forms of truth, religious or philosophical. But many are well prepared to argue the "sciences" of psychology, anthropology, and sociology as over against religion. It is not irritating to this college religion professor to find sophomores, after their first acquaintance with Freud, rise in class and dramatically challenge me to refute "his" thesis that my belief in God is a hangover from my Oedipus complex. But it is quite shocking to me to find mature adults assuming that psychology alone has all the answers, explanations, and tests of truth. Today, psychology has become a religion for many, just as experimental science was the cure-all a hundred years ago. Since the apparently conflicting claims of science and religion, of reason and faith, remain a substantial barrier to an understanding of religion, I believe that the problem must be discussed in some detail at this juncture. It is appropriate to examine first the barrier.

A. *Science*

Just what is science? What does it do and how does it operate? Why do we believe it conflicts with religion? The latest trend in science, which is not without challenge, views the enterprise in the following way. There are two main parts of science.

1. *Experimental science.* The first part is called experimental science and, as the name implies, it concerns itself largely with experiments. This enterprise uses the method of observation, measurement, and experiment on objects of nature, such as animals, rocks, trees, liquids, etc. Experiment is thus usually confined to natural objects or phenomena, though some is done on humans as in laboratory medicine (analysis of blood, gland, tissue secretions, and cells, etc.).[1] This method is pursued by the use of certain tools—tools for observation like the human eye, microscopes, cameras, spectroscopes; tools for measurement—of speed, weight, density, length, numbers; tools for special experiments—test tubes, vacuums, chemicals, etc. In addition, the method involves controlled experiments with special tools for the special situation. To use a simple example, we might want to know how much weight an iron bar two inches in diameter could hold without bending. We can easily arrange an experiment which will give us the desired knowledge. All we have to do is to place a two-inch iron bar on two supports, suspend a platform from the middle of the bar, and then load the bar with known weights until it begins to bend. To do this we have to use certain tools: correct weights, some kind of measuring tool which will tell us the moment the bar bends even if we can't see it with our eyes. Thus, even for this experiment, many instruments and operations are involved. We can use only certain kinds of tools and these tools must themselves be accurate and we trust that they are.

Experimental science, thus, deals largely with natural objects whch can be easily observed, measured and tested by certain tools. The information discovered by this aspect of

[1] This description may seem unduly narrow in view of the obvious fact that the experimental method is used widely in analyzing human behavior patterns. Recent attempts are even applying this method to the social sciences. Our description is here narrowed somewhat artificially in order to view the method in one of its purest forms.

science is usually exact, reliable and precise for these reasons: (1) its objects are capable of being controlled and measured by mathematically accurate standards; (2) whatever activity is present in the objects occurs again and again in exactly the same way, or, if different, the variation can be clearly seen by the same tools; (3) no emotional or subjective factors in the observer have the slightest effect on the experiment. Or, to put it the other way around, the conditions of the experiment and its objects do not in any way depend upon the emotions, feelings, beliefs of the scientist. Yet the scientific observer as a person is involved in the experiment. He has to use his own sense experience to observe data, his imagination to devise new experiments, his memory to retain observed images, and his reason to relate data to laws or to form new concepts. Of course, it is expected that he will leave out whatever other personal factors he may have, such as private prejudices and emotions. Experimental science, in its most precise use, deals primarily with natural objects which are capable of being controlled and measured by certain tools. It deals with what is repeatable, constant and common. It is, indeed, a magnificent enterprise which has produced incalculably valuable information to mankind and has resulted in producing invaluable inventions and knowledge which have enabled us to combat more successfully disease, the forces of nature, and many of the hazards of living. But, of course, this part of science cannot and does not do everything. In fact, it is very dependent upon another branch of science.

2. *Theoretical science.* Theoretical science, as its name implies, concerns itself more with theories than with particular experiments. It uses most of the methods and much of the data of experimental science, but then goes beyond this to classify and predict the properties and activities of natural phenomena. In addition, it constantly re-examines the hypotheses and the tools used in experimental science as well

as the data which are produced. New information and new discoveries often throw new light on old problems and require scientists to revise some of their theories or develop new and more accurate tools. It is the job of the theoretical scientist to discover the theoretical bases for new experiments and to evaluate the significance of new information in its relation to old information. Of course, a scientist does not have to be either an experimentalist or a theorist; he is frequently both. Today, however, the theoretical field has become so important that many leading scientists devote themselves almost entirely to that aspect of science. That theory is of prime importance in science, as it has been in other kinds of human activity, and was dramatically recorded in the history of the discovery of atomic fission. Atomic energy was not discovered and controlled merely by a series of trial and error laboratory experiments. For a long time, the chief barriers to its successful production were intricate technical problems which could be solved only by recourse to highly abstract theories known only to skilled theoreticians. Indeed, laymen might well be bewildered and surprised if they visited some of the distinguished scientists at work in a place like the Institute for Advanced Study at Princeton. Here one would find a great physicist or mathematician staring at a blackboard filled with apparently unintelligible symbols and figures. At first, one might well wonder whether such a scientist provides society with any useful or practical contribution. Yet, the answer is obvious. Without them, we would be living in primitive times. Most of the everyday conveniences and necessities, like electricity, water power, heat, automobiles, medicines, were made possible only by repeated testing of an originally "impractical" theory.

Theoretical science thus is really the basis of all scientific activity. It re-examines hypotheses and evaluates the accuracy of tools. It tries to arrive at general laws which help us to make predictions about how things will operate. And, by the inductive method of thinking, it tries to arrive at some general knowledge of everything experienced in the world of nature. Theoretical science, as Whitehead has suggested, is primarily concerned with abstractions. To the layman, these abstract ideas are just as obscure and seemingly irrelevant as abstract ideas in philosophy and theology. Yet, without this aspect of science, the other activities of science would stumble along with very little progress. On the other hand, it should be clear that theory is also dependent on data. This is why theoretical and experimental science are indispensable to each other and constitute what is meant by the enterprise of science.

The question of the branches of science can be raised here. Psychology, sociology, anthropology, etc., are not essentially different sciences. They are scientific in the sense that they apply the scientific method to special fields such as the human mind and body, the social aspects of humans, and animal growth and behavior. Natural science is a term used to cover the areas in which experimental science has always labored— physics, chemistry, biology, geology, etc. In short, all branches of science are the same because they use the same method. They differ only because their fields of interest vary.

This designation of the method and tools of science and the objects of the study has neglected the limitations of the method. Science is limited first of all by its method—the observation and control of experiments. There are many things in life which cannot be entirely "observed." A cause is occasionally assumed because of some effect even though the cause cannot be clearly identified. Some types of energy are difficult to discover—motion sometimes has to be inferred because of a change of position. These are some of the limitations of science within its own sphere of interest.

It is obvious that human ideas cannot be seen either by the

eye or by instruments. Values cannot be controlled in the laboratory. Hopes and fears cannot be tested. The method of science was not designed for these aspects of life and it cannot deal with them. Because the scientific method cannot observe some types of energy and causes, or ideas and values, it would be foolish to conclude that, therefore, these things do not exist. Similarly, most of the tools of science are limited. The tools of the laboratory, of measurement, and all the other apparatus are special mechanisms for special jobs. They cannot be used as a yardstick for everything. A ruler will not help us to find out the weight of water, a spectrum cannot give us the value of democracy. Also, since the method and tools of science are derived from and designed for what is common and recurrent in nature, it is not equipped adequately to handle what is unique, what happens only once. Today, scientists are deeply concerned about certain events in the history of evolution, biology, and energy which are unique. Some unusual occurrence took place which led to a significant change and yet so far as is known, such an event has not yet happened again. This raises the problem of whether the method and tools are adequate and, even more important, it reduces all the laws and hypotheses to "educated guesses." The so-called "laws of science" are not absolute certainties; they are "statistical averages of high probability." That is, the laws are true most of the time and probably all of the time of our life span. But there is always the possibility of the rare exception which can occur at any time. And it would be a poor scientist who ruled out the real likelihood of some new change. The cut and dried laws of cause and effect of a century ago are under constant suspicion and criticism by the scientists of today. Life is not that simple or that mechanical. The activity of energy, the workings of cell tissue, the functioning of whole organisms with their intricate related parts, and many other aspects, still remain essentially mysterious and awesome. And most great scientists have a reverence and a respect for the fascinating mysteries they seek to penetrate. It is only the amateurs and sophomoric scientists who think that science deals only with provable facts. So, even in its own field, science is limited.

It should be obvious by now that science is limited in its application to other fields of life. As has been suggested, science cannot tell us much about values, morals, right, and wrong. Whether one should give money to charity or not is not a scientific problem. Science cannot give one much help in deciding whether one will lie or not, or how one should vote on a certain economic measure. To be sure, some scientific information may help one to make a judgment about some things, but in the last analysis, the decision is not a scientific one but a moral or religious one.

Similarly, science cannot tell one about the meaning of life —whether it is worth living. It cannot tell a person the meaning of tragedy and evil, and if faced with these, why he should try to endure them. Science cannot make one either an optimist or a pessimist about life, or about one's fellow man. It cannot prove or disprove God, faith, or the content of religious doctrine. These problems are not scientific problems and, therefore, the method of science cannot be fully applied; other methods and tools have to be used. Just because science cannot determine the truth or error of these problems does not mean that they do not exist. Or, to turn the issue around, if a religionist said that his religion could not discover the presence of the pituitary gland and that, therefore, no such gland existed, a scientist would rightly protest. He would say that the method and tools of religion are not designed to discover such things. Yet, how many people today use the argument that because God cannot be proved scientifically, there is no God? If the nature of science is really understood, this type of thinking should be eliminated. Science is one of the greatest of all enterprises and achievements of man, but the business of living and life itself is still bigger than science. We need all the science we can get, but we still need all the philosophy and religion we can get. Science need not be a barrier to religion, but rather an open door.

B. *Philosophy*

In the past, philosophy has sometimes been a barrier to the understanding of religion. Before the days of modern science, many people believed that the method of philosophy was the sole avenue to truth. All things had to be subjected to and tested by rational coherence, or logic, or understanding. Whatever could not be fitted into these forms was often regarded as untrue or non-existent. Since many of the discoveries of science and many of the beliefs of religion could not be described or proved in some philosophical manner, both science and religion suffered some heavy attacks from the philosophers. It is ironic that today the majority of philosophers are somewhat servile spokesmen for science. However, the philosophic giants of the past, like Aristotle, Plato, and Kant, were not against science or religion *per se*. They tried to fit all knowledge into some coherent and understandable system. And this brings us to the nature of philosophy.

Philosophy is man's attempt to organize his various experiences, scientific data, and religious truth into some rational system. It represents man's search for truth, using all knowledge that is available to him, and trying to make it all unified and understandable. To do this, philosophy has a set of tools and a method. It has no mechanical tools, no laboratory, no controlled experiments. Its laboratory is the mind; its tools are logic, concepts, and reason; and its method is reflective thought and analysis. Whatever truth in life can be discovered by this method is the province of philosophy. Philosophy is thus the search for truth insofar as truth can be discovered by reason and the mind. From this, it should be clear that philosophy cannot arrive at all knowledge. It cannot discover the truth that science finds, nor can it dig up the truth that religion claims. But philosophy, like science, is indispensable. It is the great and necessary critic of all human activity. Because it takes the information which all enterprises provide and tries to relate and systematize these truths, it seeks to achieve a more complete view of life and of truth itself. Particularly in this age of super-specialization, where most of us know only our own special interests, philosophy helps us to integrate our knowledge with the data discovered by other specialists. The philosopher is the great synthesizer for he tries to see how all facets of life fit together. He is trying to find an intelligible pattern to life. He hopes that life is a kind of magnificent tapestry composed of many fine and variable strands. If one strand of knowledge tends to imagine that it is the whole tapestry, the philosopher does not agree. Though he, himself, is one of the strands, his honest and inquiring mind knows that he is but one among many—that all are important. But his great passion is to discover the pattern of the whole tapestry, how each strand fits in with others to make a unified harmonious whole.

Philosophy, thus, is man's great search for unified truth. And yet it, too, is limited. We have said it cannot discover either scientific or religious truth. But it can say whether the truths of science and religion are coherent with other truths already known, or whether they are subject to rational analysis. It can say how these truths fit or do not fit into some philosophical system. But again, philosophy, like science, cannot discover and test all truth. And it is not fair to say that because some things cannot be proved by the method of philosophy that, therefore, they do not exist or are not true. Philosophy cannot say whether the chemical properties of sugar are poisonous or not. Philosophy cannot tell whether John Smith is really in love with Susie Jones or whether it is puppy love. And philosophy cannot say whether there is a God or is not a God, and if there is, whether he is a terrible tyrant or a righteous, yet loving, God. Philosophy, then, is another magnificent and invaluable enterprise in life. Many people are intellectual schizoids; that is, they have a vast amount of information, but it is not organized into a pattern or tapestry. An appreciation of the discipline of philosophy would help all of us out of our present confusion, departmentalization of facts, and fuzzy thinking.

C. *Theology*

Thus far, we have seen that science concerns itself primarily with natural phenomena, and philosophy with reflective, systematic thought. Theology is still another enterprise which concerns itself with a third area of life—the area of God's activity. Theology begins with God. It does not begin by asking whether there is a God or not, and then sets out to prove it one way or another. Theology starts from the premise that there is a God. Its function, therefore, is to describe the nature and activity of God, and His relationship to man and life in general.

Many people feel that theology is doomed from the start because it begins with an assumption—there is a God. "That's the trouble with religion—it starts with something that can't be proved, only assumed." This criticism has annoyed some religionists to the extent that a few eager, contemporary theologians have attempted to show that theology does not begin from this assumption but begins on a fact that can be scientifically or empirically demonstrated. This seems to me to be an error. For not only theology but also science and philosophy begin with some initial premise. Science assumes that there is a world of nature and that human beings can have an accurate knowledge of phenomena. Science does not begin by saying, "Maybe there are natural objects and maybe there are not. Maybe we just *think* there are, but maybe it is only perverted images in our minds. Therefore, let us first set out and prove that the objects are there and that there is a one to one correspondence between our images and the objects." Science does not do this. It assumes the existence of phenomena. That is why it can be said that the concept of science is not a scientific concept. It is a philosophical one. For the whole problem of how one can know anything outside himself is a philosophical one. That it is a major problem is indicated by the pretentious title given to it—epistemology—the theory of knowledge. The point here, however, is that science begins with an assumption which cannot be proved scientifically.

Similarly, philosophy begins with a premise. Philosophy starts from the assumption that reason can find truth, that there is truth to be found, that it not only can be found, but can be rationally described and communicated. Philosophy does not begin by saying, "We do not know if there is any truth or not, or whether we can find it if there is." Long ago, the great philosopher Plato saw the impossibility of solving that problem by philosophy. Briefly, he put it something like this: If we don't know what the truth is, then how can we go look for it? And if we know what the truth is, then we've already got it so we don't have to look for it. Thus, we cannot look for something when we don't even know what it is we are looking for. So philosophy cannot be established philosophically either. It, too, has to start from an assumption; namely, that there is truth and even though we don't know what it is now, we *can* know it by reason—at least partly. This is where philosophy starts. Likewise, theology starts with its assumption: that there is a God and that He can be known. I do not see how science, philosophy, or theology can ever escape the necessity of an initial assumption. All three enterprises, then, have some initial faith, some assumed starting point which can be tested again and again in various types of experience, but which can never be absolutely proved.

In stating, therefore, that theology begins with a premise, I am not putting into theology anything that isn't also present in science and philosophy. Theology assumes, then, that there is a God and that God has acted or revealed Himself in a person, or persons, in nature, and in history. The Hebrews did not imagine some idea of God and then because they thought it was such a clever idea, decide to accept it. God acted upon them in their experience, and their theology is the attempt to describe and interpret this activity as a revelation of the nature of God. Thus, in a real sense, theology is partly derived from experience. But it is not totally derived from experience since it has to interpret experience. This means that in a given religious experience, the person has an intense awareness that the experience is not merely biological, or psychological, or sociological—but also religious. That is to say, the person feels he is now aware of *another* area of reality, an area which seems to be beyond the natural world of things, or everyday psychological responses, or run-of-the-mill social experiences. It may include all these aspects; it usually does, but there is something more. Theology is the description of this "something more." This is the area of the non-natural, the unseen, the timeless, the eternal.

In order to discover truth in this area, theology has its methods and its tools, designed to fit the subject matter. Theology uses part of the scientific method when it takes a general principle or axiom and analyzes various experiences. In the late medieval period, theology was often called "The Queen of the Sciences." For at that time, both science and theology used the deductive method; that is, one starts with general laws or theories and from these principles one analyzes particular experiences or events and thereby seeks to understand, interpret, and classify them. Today, however, most modern science, while it still uses the deductive method, uses far more frequently the inductive method. This means that the scientist attempts to formulate general laws by an examination of many events. He does not start with a law; he starts by observing certain events. When the event happens the same way again and again, he then can make a general law.

Modern theology also uses this inductive method but not as widely as science. At any rate, theology uses the scientific method of observing, classifying and interpreting various human experiences. It also uses the method of theoretical science when it deals with abstractions. Doctrines, after all, are in part abstract ideas or statements of belief. And this leads also into the method of philosophy. Theology obviously has to use the philosophic method of reflective and critical thought. Philosophical theology is the attempt to make doctrinal beliefs coincide with rational order and to fit them into some intelligible, whole pattern. Naturally, a theologian has to use his mind, his reason, his analytical and thinking processes just as the philosopher. So here, too, theology uses the same method as philosophy.

In addition, however, theology must go still further and make use of another function which is called faith. We have seen that science and philosophy require some faith, in that trust in their basic assumptions is necessary. Theology has to have this kind of trust or faith, too. But it must also have another kind of faith, which is not just the acceptance of a proposition, but is an active personal relationship with a power that has personal consequences. This is faith in God. And this will be described more fully later. But here it should

be noted that Christian theology requires an active relationship between man and God. Otherwise, one could say that
without this kind of faith, the theology would be seriously
limited and would be, in effect, philosophy. There is a vast
difference between faith in *ideas about* God and faith *in* God.
I would say that philosophy can deal adequately with ideas
about God—as it has done so in the past. But only theology
can describe what God *is* and *does*. For this reason, a theologian, unlike a scientist and a philosopher, cannot be outside
the subject matter. A real theologian is necessarily involved
in religion; he cannot be neutral and then coldly examine
a religion and decide for or against it. Why this is so, we
shall try to explain in the section on faith. Perhaps an analogy will tide us over, meanwhile. A foreigner can learn a
good deal about America by reading a lot of books about us.
But he cannot really obtain a full understanding of our country and what *we* are like until he comes over here and lives
in America. The same holds true to Christianity. One can
learn a lot *about* it, but he does not really know and fully
understand it until he is *in* the faith.

The method of theology, therefore, uses the scientific and
philosophic method insofar as these methods can be used, and,
in addition, uses the method of faith—an active relationship
with God. Theology also has its tools, specially designed for its
field. Some of its tools are like those of science in that theology has general principles and abstractions, some are like philosophy in that the powers of the mind and reason are used,
some are like both enterprises in that memory, imagination,
sense-experience are used. In addition, special emphasis is
often put on awareness, intuition, inspired insight, and meditation. This is not to say that these tools are not also used by
the scientist or philosopher, for they often are. What is suggested here is that these aspects of human beings point to faculties of knowing which are not specifically or completely ra-

tional or mechanical. These ways of knowing are extra-sensory
and extra-rational. And everybody uses these faculties. Many
common expressions describe what is meant here: "I knew
in my *heart* that it would turn out this way," "I just had a
feeling that this would happen," "I know in my *bones* it's
going to rain tomorrow," "I never understood that until it
dawned on me suddenly." These everyday happenings indicate how some things are learned. Much of this type of learning is probably the result of unconscious concerns rising into
our conscious awareness. *How* this occurs varies, and the
point is simply that this process is one of the many ways we
learn things and it is not a purely rational process. Religion
uses this tool or process a great deal. If any religion ever used
only this tool, it would be an extraordinarily dangerous religion. Similarly, if any scientist used only one or two tools,
he might not be dangerous, but he certainly would be piti-
fully ineffective.

Theology, philosophy, and science, then, are similar in
many ways, and their differences are both healthy and necessary, for each is concerned with some great area of life. Conflict between them seems to me to be unnecessary and wrong.
In the past, almost all the conflicts have been due to over-
zealous, if not arrogant, proponents who imagined that their
enterprise was the *sole* avenue to truth, or that their one
area was the whole of life. Fortunately, the trend today is
toward closer harmony and cooperation, or, as one great
mathematician-philosopher has put it, "The dogmas of religion are attempts to formulate in precise terms the truths
disclosed in the religious experience of mankind. In exactly
the same way, the dogmas of physical science are attempts to
formulate in precise terms the truths disclosed in the sense
perception of mankind." [1]

[1] A. N. Whitehead, *Religion in the Making;* Macmillan, New York,
1926: p. 58.

D. *The Function of Reason in Religion*

There are several views on the place of reason in religion. The first view, which can be labeled an extremely rational-istic one, supposes that reason is the one way to truth. All things must be judged in the light of reason; only in this way can truth be determined. If a religious belief or a political creed is not easily proved by reason, then it must be regarded as untrue. Thus, if one said that he believed Jesus to be both God and man, the rationalist might say that this is a logical absurdity and that, therefore, the belief is not true. Or one might say that man is a victim of environment, but he is also free from environment. Logically, this is a contradiction, and a strict rationalist would say that such a statement is obviously untrue.

From some points of view, including the Christian, ex-treme rationalism leads one into trouble and error. The as-sertion that reason is the sole test of truth rests on an assump-tion or dogma that cannot be verified by reason. How can one *prove* that reason alone can find truth? This is the prem-ise from which the rationalist starts. To use his own terms, it is not logically or rationally sound to begin with a premise and then set out to prove it. By definition one could not arrive at any other conclusion. It is tantamount to wearing red glasses and then setting out to prove that everything one sees is red and could not be any other color. Reason is a great gift and extremely valuable, but it cannot be the cure-all. Reason, like everything else, is limited. Reason cannot con-trol strong emotions like love or hate or prejudices. There are aspects of truth and reality which cannot be grasped en-tirely by reason. If a religious person adopted this rational-istic position, he would reduce religion to a series of rational precepts and propositions which might satisfy the intellect but would hardly enlist the strong allegiance of the rest of the personality.

A second view of the function of reason in religion arose largely in protest against this extreme rationalistic view. This second school, in turn, tends to rule out reason in religion almost entirely. Exponents of anti-rationalism assert that reason is totally incapable either of proving or of disproving religious beliefs. Indeed, reason is more often a barrier to religion. Reason, it is pointed out, is, after all, only part of man, and, as such, it is finite and limited as is man. But more important than that, reason is corrupted and perverted by man's self-interest and selfishness. Rationally, man knows he ought to do this and that, but the fact is he does not often do it. Desires and emotions, passions and lust overpower reason. And this school borrows a lesson or two from modern psychology to support its view. It emphasizes the now well-known process of rationalization in which one uses reason to justify what he suspects cannot or should not be excused! At any rate, for people holding this view, reason has virtually little importance in religion. For reason has nothing to say about the *truth* of any given Doctrine of God, Grace, Salvation, and Christ. The most that reason can do is to say whether the formulations of beliefs are logical and rationally set forth, but it cannot deal with the basis and content of the beliefs.

A third view of reason might be called the "middle-ground school." The most famous exponent of this view was probably St. Thomas Aquinas. He held that reason is given to all men as a natural endowment and that it is *not* corrupted by self-interest (sin). By the exercise of his reason, man can discover and prove the existence of God and much of His nature. There are other aspects of God and religion, however, which reason cannot find. Grace, God's mercy and forgiveness, can be known only through faith. Reason, however, can carry man well along the road to truth and religion, and where reason stops, faith begins and carries on to the end. There is no necessity for disagreement between reason and faith. Both are necessary and complement each other. What faith appropriates is not irrational or contrary to reason, it is merely added to reason. Indeed, the truths of faith are not at all irrational, St. Thomas would say, but are indeed rational, even though they cannot be discovered first by reason. So in this view, reason is used first and faith is added unto it.

A fourth view of the place of reason in religion is, I believe, the historic and classical Christian view. This judgment is, of course, made from my own religious and theological background. Roman Catholics, from their background, naturally regard St. Thomas' view as the "historic" traditional Christian position. This cannot be argued here. At least, this fourth view is most certainly present throughout Christian history, and it is the one that seems to me to have been shared by the greatest number of distinguished Christian theologians. From Justin Martyr through Augustine, who was its greatest exponent, to Luther and Calvin, this view has been stated repeatedly, and it finds many adherents today.[1]

The classical Christian view asserts that reason is not God, it is not the sole criterion of truth, and it not only finite and limited, but often corrupted by sin. Yet, it is a necessary and valuable faculty. Its great function is to serve as an instrument of criticism and as a restraint upon extreme interpretations of emotional and mystical experiences. Reason is indispensable to reflection on and analysis of various religious experiences, as well as to the task of relating them to other experiences or known principles. As has been pointed out before, theology inevitably uses reason in deduction and induction, in comparing ideas and beliefs, in classification, and in the communication of ideas to others. Thus, a high value

[1] Alan Richardson, *Christian Apologetics;* Harpers, New York, 1948.

is placed on reason. It has always been regarded as one of God's priceless gifts to man and, indeed, one of the media through which God speaks to man. But according to the classical Christian view, faith comes first. As developed later, it will be asserted that reason can operate at its fullest only when illumined by faith. For example, a man has a certain experience. Perhaps he sees a bully hurting a small child. As an observer, the man experiences considerable emotion which seems to prompt him to take action against the bully. One problem here is the nature of this emotion. His reason may analyze it from the categories already accepted. His conclusion, quite logical, might be that it was simply a response in accord with a prevailing moral code. On the other hand, he might be aware that there was something special in this experience which points beyond mere social codes because it seems to lead to the problem of whether this event is wrong regardless of particular codes. It may be significant enough for him to trust it. That is, he has faith that this experience is worth analyzing not only from viewpoints already known, but from some new standpoint. He, therefore, goes on to search for new understanding as to what this given experience means. Reason is used to determine the meaning of experience, but faith provides the impetus to search for the meaning. In addition, faith tends to enlarge the area of search. The function of reason, therefore, in the Christian religion is to act as the instrument of faith. But what is faith?

E. *Faith*

Although we have already mentioned faith, in passing, we need to examine it more in detail. For some odd set of reasons, modern man seems to equate faith with ignorance. Students still like to argue the proposition: should one have faith or not have faith? And a surprisingly large number of people believe the latter position is the easiest to defend because it is obviously the most correct position! In our age people seem to think that science deals with facts, philosophy with guesswork, and theology with things that aren't true. Therefore, certainty in life is to be found only in facts; nothing else is needed. Yet how much of everyday life is based upon assumptions which are neither facts nor criteria capable of proof! We assume that no accident will befall us today and so we make plans for the evening. But we do not know *for sure* that nothing will happen. And sometimes insurance statistics about accidents make our cocksure assumptions very tenuous indeed. Nobody can prove beforehand that a marriage will be happy, but millions get married on the premise that they can be happy. Nobody can prove that his chosen career will be successful, but he sets out on the faith that it will. Thus, we live literally by faith. Nearly all decisions have this basic element of faith in them. There is very little in life about which one can be completely certain. Any argument about whether man can live by faith or not is strictly an academic one. The only real argument is *which* faith will one adopt?

The Christian faith is the concern here. First, let it be said what the Christian faith is not. It is not an idea about God, nor is it the passive acceptance of some dogmas, nor submission to some intellectual proposition. Faith is not a substitute for reason or science, either. No responsible Christian theologian has ever claimed that faith could fill in some gap in the area of scientific or rational knowledge. If science has not yet fathomed some of the answers in the field of physics and chemistry, faith cannot provide the sought-for formula. Nor will faith supply an answer which can be supplied by rigorous thought and study. The lazy man cannot call up God on a spiritual telephone and get the answer to the homework problem that can be solved by hard study.

Faith is not a set of "quickie" answers. Finally, there is nothing in the Christian faith that provides a set of easy rules for the daily decisions all of us must make. These things have little, if anything, to do with the Christian faith.

What *is* Christian faith, then? The core of faith is an act resulting from an experience or group of experiences. It is an act which trusts the experiences as being significant and then searches out their deeper meanings. This type of action means contact with a new aspect of reality. Christian faith is, therefore, an active commitment to a way of life. It is an active relationship between this Reality, which we call God, and man. Since action is stressed here, it implies that the whole person is involved in this faith. Faith requires not the mind alone, or the heart (or emotions) alone, but the whole person with all his faculties. Hence, the Biblical emphasis: "Thou shalt love the Lord thy God with *all* thy *heart,* with *all* thy *mind,* and with *all* thy *soul.*" Furthermore, one cannot have an active relationship with a proposition or idea, any more than one can have fellowship with a tree. One does not pray to a concept called the Unconditioned or the Divine Omega. Nor could one be expected to commit himself devotedly and consequently be moved to great living by "the principle of continuity" or the "process of growth." If one is to have any real personal relationship with reality, it must involve some kind of intimate, personalistic qualities. In our discussion of the Doctrine of God, we shall try to elaborate this point. In essence, then, Christian faith is a dynamic activity that engages the whole personality. Concretely, it means that a person has had experiences which have been significant. Analysis and comparison of these significant experiences with experiences of other people reveal similarity, even identity. Other people, throughout history, have described these experiences and have labeled them "religious" or "spiritual," and have then described them in detail and described also the content, object, or power present in such experiences. From this descriptive activity, one acquires the label God or Christ, or other labels from other religions. What then appears is an almost universal testimony to an experience and relationship between man and a reality that is beyond man, regardless of how it or He may work in and through man. "The relationship of men to God remains fundamentally the same, although the intellectual formulations of it change considerably." [1]

Faith is the name given to this viable relationship between man and Reality, and theology is the attempt to describe and explain it. A new experience revealing a new dimension of life leads one to trust it sufficiently to pursue its fuller significance. This new "discovery" often seems to shed new light on things we already know. One sees things from a new perspective. A broader pattern or tapestry is given. For this reason, the oft-spoken phrase "blind faith" seems to me to be a contradiction in terms. Faith is not blind; it is precisely the opposite. It is an experience of some new truth, new insight, new meaning, which lights up other truths whose connections with each other we could not see before.

This type of discovery occurs even on the level of science. For example, medical science has long known of various bodily diseases such as tuberculosis, stomach ulcers, various infections. More recently, the science of psychiatry has discovered various mental illnesses, such as neuroses and psychoses of many kinds. Only very recently, however, have relationships between physical and mental illnesses been emphasized. For a number of years, the diseases of the body and mind were known and treated separately. It was only through some new experiences and new experiments that the new knowledge was obtained. The discoverers of this new knowledge trusted these new experiences as being significant

[1] Richardson, *op. cit.* p. 90.

and then went on in the faith and hope that analysis of these experiences might lead somewhere. It did—to psychosomatic medicine. This new active and committed pursuit shed new light on some old facts.

Thus, in religion faith is not blind; it is the source of a new light and understanding. Or, as it has been described by Alan Richardson: Faith is like a new pair of glasses. One sees all the same things he saw before he got the glasses, but now he sees them in their correct proportion, as they really are. The glasses correct vision, prevent distortion, literally give new sight. Faith is thus a new way of seeing things, a new perspective. For these reasons the classic Christian statement of the role of faith was well described by Augustine, "We must first believe in order to understand."

Christianity believes that reason alone is blind, for reason must have some starting point, some category or premise. Reason, when left to itself, can only doubt and end in complete scepticism, even about itself. The sad state of much contemporary philosophy is witness to this condition. The reluctance of some contemporary philosophers to free themselves from cautious scepticism, or launch out on new adventures, new faiths, points to the stagnating quality of unaided reason. This was why Paul accused the Greeks in his day, a period of philosophic decline, as "the blind leading the blind." And today, many philosophers in America still prefer to avoid many issues for fear of being caught out on a philosophical limb. There are hopeful signs, however, that this age of impotent anxiety is nearly over.

It is the Christian faith that faith is not only a starting point, but also a continual guide to reason. From the new light of faith, a new perspective on reality is gained, and from that point on, *reason is a necessary guide*. Not to use reason after faith is to see that faith wither away, and reason decay into irresponsible cynicism. That is why one of the earliest Christian theologians (Justin Martyr) could say that faith enables a man to become *fully* rational.

We will do well, then, to put away our childish notions about the Christian faith. Faith in this religion is dynamic, derived partly from personal experience and partly from the deductions and experiences of others. It is an active commitment to a new aspect of Reality, to God. It is a real relationship which affords us new insight and understanding. It is a new way of seeing things. It does not seek after miracles or ecstatic visions, or suggest that reason be discarded. Rather, it seeks to grow, to understand more fully the glimpse of truth already seen. "We must first believe in order to know."

3

REVELATION

REVELATION is one of those theological terms that seem to frighten people away from religion, especially from Christianity. Many people have heard that revelation is a key word in the Christian faith and that if you don't believe in it, you can't be a Christian. And revelation to most of these people seems to mean something dark and mysterious, or miraculous and dramatic. What is worse, revelation appears to be something reserved only for crackpots, fanatics, and other assorted religious fools. Some alcoholic gets drunk, has hallucinations, gives his last ten dollars to charity and claims he has a revelation from God which told him to do it. The public looks on such an event as an example of Christian revelation.

Or, sometimes people look at some creed and wonder if the statements are revealed by God and therefore unalterably true. Since the Church puts so much stock in creedal statements, many think the Church claims they are the product of revelation. On the other hand, many people find descriptions of revelation which seem to be obscure, confused, and highly subjective. Or, as one professor said, "The trouble with revelation in Christianity is that when it happens to somebody, he can't tell anybody else what it was all about. So what good is it if it remains something indescribable, ineffable and esoteric?" And so it goes.

38

It is quite true that revelation is central to the Christian faith, and it is one of the doctrines which distinguishes Christianity from all other religions. It is also true that revelation is probably the most misunderstood of all the Christian beliefs. Let us see if some of the misunderstandings can be straightened out. First, it must be made clear what revelation is not! It is not any of the things described in the preceding paragraph. Revelation is not an hallucination produced by alcohol, gin, cocaine or other manufactured, chemical spirits. Secondly, it is not creedal statements or theological doctrines, nor is it something which happens to one person, but cannot be communicated to another. Revelation is never some divine proposition handed down by God. God does not, with a moving finger that writes upon the wall, give us some statement about Himself and then throw a couple of lightning bolts at us in order to scare us into believing it. Revelation, in Christianity, is never an idea or a proposition or a theological doctrine. As was explained earlier, *all* theological statements and beliefs are the results of *man's* attempt to describe religious experiences and are therefore limited, as are all human statements. Christian men write theology; God does not. God is not a magical, tyrannical theologian who hands us dogmas and then frightens us into accepting them. Thirdly, revelation in Christianity does not fill in the gaps in human knowledge. That is to say, in the realm of science, of philosophy, some mysterious problem or event cannot be solved by revelation. For example, not a great deal is known about glands, and less is known about virus infections. Medical men would like to know more about these things and are constantly seeking to find the answers. Such answers have not been found. And they never will be found by religion or revelation. No beseeching God with bargains or petitions will evoke some dramatic revelation. Those mysteries are in the field of medical science and they will be resolved only by medical scientists. Revelation is not the plug that fills in all the gaps in human knowledge.

In the field of religion and ethics, revelation is no filler. Many naive but often sincere folk say, "I had a revelation which told me to help Susie," or to vote democratic, or to be a pacifist. God does not make decisions for us; he does not lead us around by our spiritual noses. Again revelation is none of these things.

What, then, *is* revelation? Revelation is God revealing Himself, His own nature, in power, order, love, righteousness, glory. Now what does all that mean? Christian theologians say that God reveals Himself in two main ways. The first is called general revelation. This is the idea that God is present in the order of history, and in the actions of all men everywhere. This is perhaps best seen in the various religions of mankind. There is a universal religious consciousness in all of mankind. This can be seen by the countless forms of worship, gods, religious symbols, religious ethics.[1] It is also evidenced in the passionate search for truth as seen in philosophy and science. All men seek some meaning in and understanding of life, and this quest for meaning is what is meant by religious consciousness. Christian theology believes this to be a basic part of man, and this part is labeled, "the image of God" (*imago dei*). What Christianity is trying to say here is that God has made man so that he tries one way or another to seek Him. We are not complete until we live in contact with Him. Augustine described the sense of incompleteness in his famous sentence, "Our hearts are restless until they find their rest in Thee" (*Confessions,* Book I).

The word "image" is important here and it is used

[1] See William James, *Varieties of Religious Experience;* Longmans, Green, New York, 1922.

throughout Christian theology. As the word implies, an image is not the same thing as God Himself. When you see yourself in a mirror, you are viewing an image. What is in or on the glass is not you; it is an image of you. Yet if you were not existing, present, there would be no image. This distinction is important because many moderns believe there is part of God in each person, a "divine spark," a small "flame." And God, therefore, is the sum of all the sparks. Historic Christian theology does not hold to this view. God is more than the sum of the parts or sparks, and God is not really *in* given individuals, residing there as part of the person. His image only is there in all men. This image is the spiritual restlessness of men. As will be seen in the chapter on the Doctrine of Man, it is that part of human nature which is not subject to nature, but is what is meant by our spiritual nature. The image of God in men seeks the reality which produces the image. Our spirits, then, are like the image in the mirror which points to the cause of the image. General revelation, first of all, is the idea that God's image is present in all men. "So God created man in his own image, in the image of God created he him" (Genesis 1:27). God has planted a restlessness in us which will always be dissatisfied until it finds its creator—God.

Secondly, general revelation also means that God is the creator and sustainer of life. In saying that God is the creator of life, theologians do not intend to argue with the science of evolution and biology. Christians are not so naive as to believe in the fable of the stork who brings babies. Nor do Christian theologians maintain that the biblical account in Genesis is the actual scientific statement of how the universe was created. All the latest accounts of evolution and biology on these matters are accepted. But after this has been done, there are still some questions which are not answered by scientific accounts. These questions are: Where did life come from originally? Who or what created it? Since there seems to be a considerable amount of order and design, and perhaps purpose behind nature and life, where did this come from, who or what created it? And *what* purpose? These are religious questions and can only be answered by some kind of religion. There are many answers. Some would say these questions cannot be answered. It is true; they cannot be answered—scientifically. But that doesn't mean there aren't any answers. An honest scientist will simply say, "Scientifically, I don't know," and leave the door open. Only a narrow dogmatist—be he scientist or philosopher—would say, "There is no design or purpose or creator or God, and these are irrelevant and foolish questions." Christian theologians believe these are crucial questions and answer them by asserting that it is the Christian faith that God is the creator of life, that He is the sustainer in the sense that the process of life seems to be continuous, orderly, with some degree of design and purpose, and indeed meaningful. Life makes sense, wonderful sense. It is the Christian faith that God created all of life and created it in such a way that it is an orderly process, going somewhere, to some great fulfillment or purpose. Christians do not believe in God and also in a natural process which is a series of meaningless accidents, chances, and quirks of fate. When someone uses the word "chance" or "coincidence" or "accident," it can be pointed out that such words are not real explanations, but confessions of ignorance. All they really mean is "I don't know." Therefore, the honest thing to do would be to say at once, "I don't know," rather than to discuss the possibility of other explanations by a dogmatic "It's pure chance, man. Don't hand me any religious nonsense."

On the other hand, Christian theology does not use the

idea of design and order in life as a proof of the existence of God. This has been a traditional argument in philosophy. But as other philosophers have shown, one cannot rationally prove the existence of God by saying that since there is purpose or order in life ergo there must be somebody who created it. Christians believe this to be true, but they do not try to prove God's existence by argument, logical or scientific. General revelation means here that behind the origin of life, behind the order and purpose that can be seen in nature, there is a sustaining and powerful Reality which is called God.

Thirdly, general revelation is also the idea that there is a moral order behind history. The stream of events in history, with nations rising and falling, empires and tyrannies coming and going, is not due merely to political, economic, and psychological causes. In addition, Christians believe there are moral causes. Right and wrong do make a difference in life. Christians do not believe that a tyrant can rob, murder, exploit, conquer, and "get away with it." It is the Christian faith that life is so built that man cannot long commit all kinds of obvious evils and have nothing happen to him. "Crime does not pay" is the old adage. Christian doctrine states that crime does not pay in the long run. The idea that behind obvious historical events there is a moral order to history, an order which is just as real and operative as natural laws, is the great contribution of the Old Testament prophets—Amos, Isaiah, Jeremiah, Ezekiel. Thus, general revelation also means that there is a moral structure of life.

These things, then, are what Christian doctrine means by general revelation. Revelation means God revealing Himself as active in general ways, as an image in all men, as the creator of the life force, as the reality or sustainer of the order and purpose of nature, as the guarantor of the moral structure of history. This is a far cry from saying that God works miraculously by throwing thunderbolts and floods around in order to scare people into church. It is a far cry from saying that there is part of God in everybody, in trees and flowers, in sunsets, music, mountains, and purple cows. God is none of these. God is what created the process in which these things live. And Christians believe it to be an orderly, purposeful, and moral universe.

The other main way God reveals Himself is described as special revelation. Christian doctrine asserts that in addition to general revelation, God also reveals Himself especially in relatively few events, or persons, and usually at a definite time and place in history. According to Christian doctrine, for example, God revealed something of His nature through the great prophets of the Old Testament. This does not mean that every single word or deed of the prophets was the full activity of God. It means that the great "insights" of the prophets were God speaking through them to man. For it was from the prophets that we learned about God as the Lord of History, a righteous, moral God who had created a structure of life which rapacious nations were violating. These nations were an "embarrassment to God," so to speak. The Hebrews were a small nation caught between two great nations, Egypt on one side, Babylonia (later Persia and Assyria) on the other. Israel was a kind of political football kicked around by great empires. The Hebrews wondered if this constant subjugation and warfare were just accidents or a series of unfortunate "chances." Was all of history, of life, really just a series of wars and tragedies? The prophetic answer, or rather God's answer through the prophets, was "No." In spite of all these things, life is not meaningless, it is meaningful. Why? Because God, not Egypt or Israel or Babylonia, is the Lord of History. History is therefore moral in structure. It is important to note that God's answer was not a specific answer to a specific question. God did not say that Israel would not suffer war again, or that Egypt would fall in twenty-six and a half months at 4:00 P.M. God revealed only something of His nature; namely, that He was behind the order of history. There is a moral structure to life. This type of revelation is called special because it occurred at special times in Israel's history and through special prophets. Why God chose those times and those particular prophets instead of other ones, nobody can answer.

Lastly, the most significant special revelation in Christianity is, of course, Jesus Christ. Christians believe that God revealed Himself most fully and clearly in Jesus of Nazareth. In this sense, Christ was a unique and very special revelation. Indeed, it is the Christian faith that God was in Christ, that God thereby invaded time, space, and history in the person of Christ. This idea is succinctly expressed in one of the Creeds (Chalcedonian) by the statement that Christ was "truly God, truly man," or Christ was the God-Man. What this might mean in terms of rational or scientific demonstration will be discussed later in the doctrines of God and Christ. Here, however, what is being emphasized is the affirmation that God appeared on earth and thereby revealed Himself fully and completely in the person of Jesus. This special revelation differs from the special revelation of the prophets in that God did not identify Himself in the person of the prophets, but worked *through* the prophets, *through* the words. In Christ, however, God was actually present, or, as the Gospel of John said, "And the Word (of God) was made flesh" (John 1:14). This revelation in Christ, like all other revelations, is not the disclosure of some new ideas or rules for right and wrong. Christians claim that in Christ one can see what God is like more clearly. God revealed Himself, His nature, His love, righteousness, justice, mercy, power and truth. In Christ we can see the impersonal character of God—His justice and righteousness that plays no favorites. In Christ one can also see His personal nature, His love and mercy, His Fatherhood relationship to man. The nature of God will be more fully discussed in the chapter on the Doctrine of God.

What is important to notice here is the Christian belief that Christ was the special and full revelation of God. And this is the central point of the Christian faith. This is the point from which a Christian advances into all other areas. This is the key by which one is able to unlock other special revelations and general revelation. One does not arrive at the acceptance of Christ as the God-Man by previous "proofs" of God from either philosophy or general revelation. Revelation is where one begins. As Richard Niebuhr has expressed it, Christ is the Rosetta Stone of Christianity. When archaeologists discovered all kinds of hieroglyphics in Iran, they were unable to decipher them, although they continued to find more and more material of the same kind. They were only interesting specimens of primitive people until they found the Rosetta Stone which gave them the key to translation. Then all the other stones and writings made sense. So it is in Christianity. The Old Testament may appear to be only an interesting source book for the study of history, anthropology, and sociology. But from the perspective of Christ in the New Testament, it is seen as the progressive revelation of God in the history of the Hebrew prophets. It now becomes not the "odd religious ideas of some ancient prophet," but the gradual and, at times, dramatic revelation of God through these events and people to those who have the key, the perspective of the New Testament. So it is with all of life for Christianity. That is why Christ is regarded as the center of history from which one can thereby know something of the beginning and the end of history.

It is at this point, if not before, that people almost always impatiently ask, "How do you know revelation?" And this question is usually followed by the demand that revelation be proved by some easy text. There is no need to doubt the sincerity of the questioner. But the subject matter at hand does not make it possible to answer the question by any easy argument. The request to prove revelation implies that it is subject to easy, rational demonstration, or explicable by reference to some clear-cut experience. Such is not the case. For, it was said earlier that revelation is God revealing Himself. And God cannot be proved by something else. If one could test God by reason or sense experience, then God would be less than reason and experience. God would simply be one of many objects brought to the bar of examination. Since God is the content of revelation it cannot be tested by something else. So while our demand for some readily knowable test of revelation is a normal and natural one, it cannot be satisfied on our terms.

How, then, do we know revelation? It is known only directly and by itself. That is to say, God is known only directly in a person-to-person relationship, between God and Man. It is much like love. One can learn a little bit *about* love by reading books and seeing other people who claim they are in love. But one still does not know what love is really like until he is *in* love in a person-to-person relationship. Yet one of the most insistent demands of young people is to have some test of love, some proof, some easily known criterion by which one can know for sure if his love is "the real thing." But no such sure proof can be given. Love is not proved by something else. To be sure, it is related to many parts of the personality. But none of these parts or groups of parts can offer a clear test of genuine love. In the last analysis, love is its own self-authenticating fact and it is discovered only by one person being in this special kind of relationship with another person. By common consent, this relationship is called love. And it is worthy of notice how difficult it is for mankind to describe just exactly what love is. It is a common experience, yet it is extremely difficult to transmit into words just exactly what love really *means* to a person. Similarly, with God's relationship to men. It is a common experience, yet difficult to describe to somebody else. On the other hand, it is *not* difficult to communicate with someone else who is in love, or who has experienced God. There is a community of lovers as well as a "community of saints" who can readily understand each other and what they *mean*, what their experiences of God or love are really like. The difficult problem is to convey the meaning to someone who stands outside, who has never had these experiences.

Revelation is, therefore, known directly and only by active participation in the experience. Or, to use another example, revelation is like the sun. It is known only directly. All light is from the sun (or suns); it is its own criterion not observed by reference to something else. It is self-authenticating; it is where we start. Hence the biblical analogy to light: "I am the light of the world" (John 8:12). "Revelation, like the sun, must be seen by its own light." [1]

Revelation, thus, is neither some new tidbit of truth, a second chapter added to the first, nor is it something that can be proved by rational demonstration. Revelation is not a dogmatic declaration by a tyrannical God, nor is it a capricious God mystifying man with irrational mumbo-jumbo. Revelation is the disclosure of God's own nature and purpose by Himself just as in human love one person really

[1] Richardson, *op. cit.* p. 224.

discloses his truest nature to another person in the love relationship.

This human analogy is very important because it is almost an exact replica of what Christianity means by revelation. Have we ever thought about just how we know another person? How does John really get to know Mary and eventually come to love her? Well, he could spend much time studying biology, chemistry, anthropology, psychology. No matter how much he studied, what would he know about Mary? He would know quite a lot about her as a physical and psychological human being. But he would not know much about Mary as Mary. What glandular activity does she have, what kind of behavior patterns does she have? Even to answer these questions, Mary has to talk and act if John is to reply correctly. What are her hopes, fears, desires, wants, conflicts? What are her ideals and values, sense of humor? We cannot find out these things *unless* Mary lets us find out about them. *She* has to take the initiative and tell us. And *she* decides *how much* she will tell us. In a very literal and real sense she discloses, *reveals* herself to us. If she refuses, we will find her difficult to know. Similarly, the New Testament writers stated that God took the initiative and revealed Himself through Christ (John 14:10). One knows God, understands revelation, by faith which is an active commitment, trust, and response to what is disclosed in Christ.

Because we have stressed that revelation cannot be subject to proof by reasoning, it may seem that Christianity is asking man to lay aside his critical faculties when it comes to a relationship with God. The reverse is true. Faith, as has been defined earlier in the book, necessarily involves all of one's abilities and powers. All that is being said is that no one of these factors is sufficient to grasp either love or revelation. One's reason, conscience, insight, aesthetic sense, and imagination are all points of contact between God and man. "Christian theology is a theology of the Word, and a word is essentially the address of one rational being to another." [1] God does not reveal Himself to irrational animals.

Revelation is thus a gift from God, not an achievement of man. Yet in order to grasp it, one needs all the faculties with which one is endowed. Because it is God's action and gift, it results in "something new," a new way of seeing things. Revelation is God speaking and acting, and one can know and understand this by faith, by a whole response of one's whole being.

[1] *Ibid.* p. 223.

4

DOCTRINE OF MAN

THE Christian view of man includes many ideas about man. It is necessary to try to discover the full nature of man, for I believe the problem to be one of the most crucial and important ones in all of life. As has been mentioned earlier in the section on *Beliefs,* what we believe about ourselves and our fellow man will largely determine our attitude and actions in life. If we believe that most men are little more than animals, we will probably tend to treat them as animals; push them around, use them for our own ends and satisfactions. If we believe most men to be nearly angelic, sweet, rational and kind, we will be in for some rude shocks. In all our social planning and hopes for peace, the practicality or impracticality of our plans and actions will depend, in large measure, upon our estimate of what man is like, how he operates, what his fears and motivations are, needs and satisfactions. Indeed, in almost all of our daily actions in life we are always faced with the problem of the nature of man. We are constantly anxious about our neighbors and ourselves. We repeatedly ask, "What are we?" "What makes us behave this way; why do we think that way?"

The Christian Doctrine of Man can be described in the following way. First of all, we are physical beings much like animals in that we have bodies, circulatory systems, glands, cellular growth and decay. We need food, shelter, activity, and rest. This is the obvious part of human nature. We are rooted firmly in the natural process and our physical bodies are governed by the laws of nature. In this respect, we are like animals. We cannot avoid or break without peril the laws that govern our natural bodies. We cannot avoid the death of the body; we cannot live without food. I need not elaborate here, for biology can tell us much more in detail the whole workings of the physical side of man.

Second, there is a psychological side to man. By this I mean that man has mental capacities. He has some faculty which is commonly called the mind, or the ability to think, reflect, analyze. Man has fears, hopes, and dreams. There seems to be some part of man which is the center of his capacity to respond to stimuli of various sorts, some organizing center which receives stimuli and causes responses. To be sure, there is still some debate among certain psychologists as to whether there is such a thing as the mind or not. This argument usually centers around a technical definition of "mind." It is not my purpose to settle the debate here in any technical sense. In passing, I can only say that at least in the broad sense of the term, I firmly believe that man has some kind of "mind," some kind of capacity to think, to worry, to hope, to laugh, to reflect; and this is what I mean by the psychological or mental side of man. The precise difference between the psychological life of animals and that of man cannot be discussed here either. Suffice it to say that the general and significant difference, in my opinion, centers on definitions of freedom and responsibility. I also agree that one cannot make a sharp distinction between the mental and the physical aspects of man. It seems obvious that the physical part of man greatly influences the mental part. But with the advent of psychosomatic medicine, we also know that the mental activity affects the physical activity of man. In the light of modern knowledge, it seems useless to us to debate the question. Does the body determine the mind, or the mind, the body? The answer today seems to be rather clear: neither and both! That is to say, they both influence each other. It is a kind of interaction. Moreover, just as there are laws as to how our bodies act, so, too, are there laws about our mental activities. And again, we must obey these laws or else suffer mental illness. So Christianity would accept quite readily the biological and psychological views of man insofar as they describe how we are rooted in the natural processes of life, and are subject to its laws. Christian theologians disagree with certain views of some biologists and psychologists who describe man as totally and only an animal or mechanism and nothing else. The reason for this disagreement is that Christians believe that man has a third side—what is called the spiritual side of man.

This third part of man's nature, the spiritual, is perhaps hard to define precisely and yet is easy to illustrate. The spiritual aspect of personality is reflected in the uniquely human capacity to ask questions about the meaning of life. Only human beings wonder whether life makes sense or not. Concern for values, for meanings, for order, for purpose in life reflect what Christianity means by "spiritual." In addition, the spiritual side of man is closely associated with self-consciousness and awareness. A machine is not aware of its existence, but human beings are. And self-consciousness involves some ability to criticize oneself. To do this, one must be able to get partly outside of oneself. We can stop a moment and analyze our actions. And we might say that such an action was quite clever. But then we can go on and analyze our criticism and say, "But maybe I'm kidding myself. Maybe it wasn't so clever. Maybe I'd just like to think it was clever." And then we can go still further and ask, "But why am I bothering to criticize myself at all?" And so it goes. Man seems to have the ability to get outside of himself and then look at himself. Of course we cannot do this completely. But the extent to which we can thus transcend ourselves is the extent to which we become more self-conscious, more aware of what we are.

By spirit, Christianity also means awareness. Our capacity for imagination and memory, our sensitivity to things material and non-material imply a unique structure to human nature. For by memory we can mentally live in the past, and by imagination we can mentally live in the future, or in some other place. This means that we are not creatures absolutely confined to time and space. Our bodies are, but our spirits or personalities are not. This is profoundly elaborated by St. Augustine in Book X of his *Confessions*. Christian doctrine also states that the ability of man to love reflects his spiritual character. While human love has many aspects which are closely allied with "natural process," such as its sexual roots, social influences, biological impulses, yet I do not believe love is purely these things. I believe that there is a certain amount of freedom involved in man's capacity to love. Again, this is difficult to define precisely, yet most of us know what is meant by the word "spontaneity" when applied to love. Love must have a strong element of spontaneity (freedom) in it if it is to mean anything. If human love is entirely an organic process of glandular activity, a mere series of cause-and-effect, stimuli-response functions, then most human beings have been "loving" under a gigantic illusion. Some amateur psychologists have made this charge of illusion. But it is difficult to see how this label could be verified. For the empirical evidence of millions of people seems to indicate otherwise. The very fact that man tends to resist all efforts to reduce him to a machine-like animal would seem to me to prove the existence of man's spiritual nature. Animals apparently do not mind being animals, machines seem content to be machines, but man is not content to be defined or reduced to either a complex animal or a delicate machine. Thus it is difficult to see how one could discuss the love experiences of millions of people as merely stimulus-response affairs.

Another common problem about the nature of man is that of freedom and determinism. One of the stock arguments of college sophomores is the debate as to whether man is free or determined. On this level, the arguments usually try to prove that either man is completely free or completely determined. In the history of philosophy the debate has been more sophisticated and more technical and I cannot here give a long critique of this problem. On the sophomore level, a theologian would say that the problem as debated was a false issue. We do not have to choose one side of the argument or the other. The obvious position seems to me to be the statement that man is *both* free and determined. This could conceivably be a logical contradiction, yet I believe it to be an empirical fact. It has been noted already how greatly man is determined by biological laws of growth and decay, psychological laws, social influences, and environment. These and many other influences do determine a large part of our personality, attitudes, and actions. Thus, man is greatly determined by forces within and without his person. But it has also been suggested that man is partly free, that self-consciousness, awareness, and the spirit of man are at least partly free from the control of nature. The real problem of freedom and determinism, as I see it, is to discover how much we are determined and how much we are free, in what areas of our personality, whether the area of freedom can be enlarged or not. And this is extremely difficult because we do not have accurate tools and methods for investigating the spiritual side of man. It is very easy to slide into the position of assuming that what we do know about human nature is all we need to know and that it accounts for everything. Because we do not know scientifically certain aspects of human nature, such as laughter, love, and spirit, it does not thereby follow that such aspects do not exist. To be sure, it is important to find out all the forces which would tend to determine our lives. But it is equally important to leave the door open for discovering by some other method the area of freedom and responsibility in human personality. According to Christian doctrine, I think the problem could be summed up this way: If man is completely determined by forces (inner and outer) beyond his control, then life is nonsense and there is nothing we can do about it anyway. If every man is a complete victim of forces, then there are no values, no morals, no truth, no meaning and purpose anywhere in life. Under such circumstances no one can be held responsible for anything, nor be blamed for anything. Nothing is better than something else. All are equal; everything is the same because, by definition, all men are what they are by pre-determined influences. By definition, they cannot be anything else. One could not, or should not, be excited about "issues"; there are no "issues." Russians are that way because they have been determined that way. We are determined, too, so why worry? And is not the worry itself determined? The more one analyzes the full implications of a rigid determinism, the more nonsense it makes.

On the other hand, it is equally foolish to assert that man is completely free, and he is absolutely the captain of his soul and the master of his fate. Science has given too much clear evidence to the contrary for us to hold on to that theory. Our determinist friends do have much evidence that cannot be disputed. Christians would say, therefore, that a thoroughgoing determinism is impossible and similarly a theory of complete freedom is impossible. The truth lies somewhere in between, and no enterprise has yet been able to define precisely where freedom operates and where determinism operates, or just how they overlap. Man, therefore, is an interaction of freedom and determinism.

Thus far, then, the description of human nature has been along lines that are generally acceptable to men of science, philosophy, and religion. There are exceptions, of course, and perhaps not all would accept our description of what is meant by the spiritual side of man. The label is not important; the idea is. The chief idea behind the word is that man is to some degree free and responsible for some of his attitudes and actions. But this is not the whole story of the Christian doctrine of man. The rest of the story concerns what some Christian theologians have labeled as *The Tensions of Man*.

In addition to what has been said above, Christian doctrine describes man as a very complex being because he is a bundle of conflicting forces. Man loves and hates, laughs and cries; he is good and he is bad; he is selfish and he is unselfish.[1] For every characteristic or quality we can name in man, we can always find the opposite quality. That is why the optimist and the pessimist are both wrong, from the Christian viewpoint, in their estimate of human nature. The optimist looks at all of man's good tendencies and concludes that man is essentially good; the pessimist reverses the process. These two views are too simple; they do not see the profound paradoxes and contradictions that make up man's nature. Perhaps a little chart can illustrate our point:

1. Unconscious   vs. Conscious
2. Nature   vs. Spirit
3. Finitude   vs. Infinitude
4. Self-Love   vs. Objective Love

[1] Some of the following material up through p. 86 has been taken from the author's first book: *Power for Action (An Introduction to Christian Ethics)*; Scribners, New York, 1948.

There are the basic paradoxes or conflicting forces which are present in all of us. Thanks to modern psychiatry (though the problem was known certainly as early as Plato), all of us are familiar with the fact that much of our living is determined by unconscious drives and tendencies. But we are also aware of our conscious forces. Further, sometimes our conscious desires and powers are in conflict with our unconscious forces, and sometimes not. So, too, with our second paradox. As has been noted above in the discussion of the physical, mental, and spiritual sides of man, we are rooted in nature and subject to its process, and yet we are partly free from nature. We have spiritual capacities which seem to be beyond nature and not subject to known natural laws. We ask "non-natural" questions when we ask about the meaning of life, or the process of nature itself.

Taking the third tension, we know that we are finite creatures. We know that we do not live forever; we know that we do not know all the answers about life and our world. In short, we know we are finite, limited creatures. Yet we seem to have within us some awareness of what we call infinity. Infinite means endless, unlimited. The idea of infinity itself is almost impossible to formulate. But man, in various ways, has sensed or felt the experience of endlessness. Mathematicians appreciate endless multiplication of numbers; philosophers have sensed the endless regress of cause and effect; religionists have felt the limitless expanse of the universe, which is also being suggested again by some astrophysicists. Thus, it may perhaps be said that the awareness of our infinitude indicates some awareness of what is not finite. If we were completely finite we could not know it. For example, the only reason I know I am inside a particular room of a building is because I know about other rooms, other buildings and the outdoors. But if I had been born and brought up in one room and never saw outside of that room, I should not know that this room was one among millions. I should think that the world was the one room. So we are finite creatures and yet not wholly finite.

Fourthly, we love ourselves very much (self-love), yet we also want to love other people, social movements, life itself (objective love). "Egotism" versus "altruism." This is one of the most basic tensions in man. The conflict between my own concerns and the needs or demands of other people is an endless one. In all human relations, this is perhaps our most fundamental and daily problem: my interests versus other people's interests. How much should I give in; how much should they give in to me? How much do I rationalize my self-interest in order to make it appear "moral"? How much is my neighbor pretending? Who is fooling whom?

A moment's thought, then, should make clear that all human beings have these paradoxical forces within their natures. Of course, we have many more forces, but the point is that these conflicts are the basic ones and that others are either variations of these or stem directly from them. Now it is important to note that most of the time these paradoxes are in conflict with each other. That is, our unconscious life is in conflict with our spiritual one. This does not mean that one set of forces is bad and the other good. It would be a mistake, for example, to say that all the natural forces or tendencies are bad, and the "spiritual" ones good. There is good and bad on both sides. The essential point here is that these conflicting and paradoxical forces in man produce tension. Wherever there is conflict, there is tension, whether we are talking about physics, politics, or man. Because we have these conflicts within us, we are in tension, we are anxious, restless, or insecure. This is one of the most fundamental facts about human nature: our conflicting drives, desires, appetites, forces, thoughts, and emotions, make us tense, anxious and insecure.

From this follows another fundamental fact about human nature: we do not like this tension. We not only do not like it, but we cannot stand it; we cannot "take it" for very long. So what do we do? The normal thing to do is to seek escape from such tension, and this is the chief endeavor and struggle of life—to find some security, some peace in our being. From the Christian point of view, almost all philosophies, religions, and ways of life—economic and political—represent some form of attempted escape from anxiety and tension. This is a very broad statement and therefore needs justification. What are some of man's various methods of escape?

The methods of escape can be seen by looking again at the chart of the tensions of man. Take the first tension—between the conscious and the unconscious. Mr. Average Citizen, who is anxious and restless, may seek to escape his insecurity by indulging in excessive drinking or "playing around" sexually. This amounts to a retreat into his unconscious life because, when he is drunk or emotionally excited, he is then relatively "free" from his conscious life. He is able to "forget everything." He has sloughed off his conscious life. His insecurity has driven him to a position where he can avoid conflict by pretending that there is no conscious power to conflict with his unconscious powers. Hence, no conflict, no tension—peace at last. Of course, this does not work because he can't be drunk or emotionally "lifted" all the time. The morning-after and its hangover will arrive shortly. Then he feels worse than he did before and so seeks more desperately to escape. Thus, it is a terribly vicious circle. The more he seeks to escape this way, the more insecure he becomes; therefore, the more frantic he becomes, the more frequently he seeks escape—until finally he will end in destruction, in one form or another (a psychoneurotic, chronic alcoholic, sex pervert, etc.).

For another example, look at the second tension—the conflict between nature and spirit. The modern and widely popular movement called naturalism is, from the Christian view, a highly articulate and refined escape from the problem of anxiety. Some naturalists believe that if man abides by nature and its laws, uses his intelligence to do so and to control himself and nature in an harmonious relationship, all will be well. Other more narrow naturalists regard the spiritual side of man either as an illusion or merely a subjective and therefore erroneous opinion. Indeed, belief in man's spiritual nature is regarded as only a rationalized ideology of selfish interests. Therefore, say some of the naturalists, we must "stick to the facts," to the laws and phenomena of nature. This is regarded as an escape, from the Christian point of view, because it attempts to slough off what cannot be sloughed off; namely, the questions of meaning and purpose. Whether we like it or not, man is so built that he will always ask the question, "Why?". He is so built that he cannot properly struggle and work unless he finds some sense, some meaning and purpose to his struggle. Such questions and emotions are not in nature. Most of what naturalism says about knowing facts and abiding by and controlling nature is right. But it doesn't say enough. When we get facts and laws, we still have to interpret those facts and ask what they mean and whether they are creative or destructive (good or bad) and how they shall be used. Take atomic power, for example. We need all the facts we can get about it. But how it shall be used and for what purposes is not a "natural" question. It is basically a spiritual question, for it presupposes some idea of values—of the meaning and purpose of life. Thus, naturalism is an escape because it seeks to avoid tension by pretending the spiritual side of man does not exist. If it does not exist, then there is no conflict between spirit and nature, and therefore no tension. The difficulty is that spirit does exist and is just as much a fact as nature itself. The logical outcome of naturalism, therefore, is to reduce us to scientific machines, however complex, utterly devoid of "disturbing, subjective opinions."

On the other hand, there are other forms of escape that are sometimes associated with, and present in, religion. Indeed, religion is used and perverted into an escape by many people. Many believe that our unconscious, natural, finite tendencies are all bad, while our conscious, spiritual and infinite tendencies are good. Then people seek escape into the "good side" and believe that it is possible to get rid of the "bad side." This method of escape is illustrated in what are often called "other-worldly religions." This is the view which believes that while this world is quite evil and tragic, the next world is good and heavenly. Therefore, if one has faith enough and prays, one will be "saved" and get to heaven. Within this group are many who believe one can be saved here and now, that if one does not drink, or smoke, or indulge in sex, in short, if one denies the natural man, one will be holy and pure on this earth. This is an escape because this view holds that one can be free from nature's influences. It is an escape into the "spiritual" and infinite. That this is impossible is readily seen by the fact that to believe you are free from evil and sin merely because you do not commit some obvious evil actions, is a very sinful statement, for it displays the cardinal sin of pride. More about sin and pride later. But elementary understanding of psychology and honesty with one's self would indicate that this method is an escape, and actually produces more tension. It produces more because one is anxious lest he lose his "holiness." And such anxiety shows that he is not perfectly holy.

In most oriental religions, as well as in some Greek religions, this method of escape is used. Nature, the body, finitude, are regarded as evil and undesirable. Various disciplines and practices are used whereby one is supposed either to obtain release from these forces or be able to control them. In the more profound of these views, it is recognized that only at death is escape a real possibility. Yet the influence of this view is still strong in America today and is exemplified in various groups which are labeled "perfectionist." There is a perfectionist group in religion which has been described above. There is a similar group among philosophers. Here among some thinkers, a method of escape is offered through reason. It is believed that by the cultivation and use of reason one can control emotion, passion, unconscious and natural impulses. This is the belief that one can escape to the conscious and infinite side of life, thereby reducing the conflict between these forces so that there is no tension. Here again, an elementary knowledge of one's self and psychology should make clear the futility of this method. And it is often demonstrated by the severe intensity and emotion with which a rationalist will defend his position or attack another's position.

Thus, from the Christian point of view, most of life and its various enterprises and programs represent man's desperate attempt to escape from his tension and anxiety. The tragedy is that these escapes only stimulate the original anxiety and make men all the more desperate. The further tragedy is that if man becomes too desperate, with the vast sources of power he now has, he may kill himself believing that he is saving himself.

Looking at the nature of man in an even wider perspective, Christian doctrine adds this: Man not only has these various conflicts and resulting tensions, but underlying and permeating these conflicts is this one, all-inclusive conflict—the conflict between God and Man. Man has one foot on Earth and one in Heaven, so to speak. This was partly suggested in the description of the conflict between nature and spirit. Of course, the chart is not altogether accurate. For one cannot chop human nature up into separate pieces and examine each piece by itself. In spite of man's conflicts, paradoxes, and contradictory forces, he is a total unit. That is to say, we have a certain unity of personality. Whatever tendencies and qualities a man has, they are uniquely gathered into one total unity. This totality and arrangement of forces into a totality differs in each person. That is why no one person is exactly like another. That is why it is a mistake to try to understand a person from just one point of view, whether it be from religious, psychological, or physiological criteria. We need to understand all these theories, but we also have to view a person as a whole, if we are to know him. This Christian view, now supported by many scientists of human nature who have arrived at this conclusion through their own methods, is often described as the theory of organism. In scientific terms, it means that one cannot understand fully any part of human beings without taking into account the *total* organism. It also means that the distinctions between matter and energy, body and mind, natural and spiritual process cannot be defined precisely or analyzed separately. It further means that a human being or any other organism affects its environment just as the environment partly influences the organism. Thus, to understand human beings in part or in totality, all these factors have to be considered, and some attempt must be made to understand the uniqueness and unifying elements of the personality. Taking this broad view, then, it is the Christian faith that one cannot fully understand man's nature in its completeness unless one sees him as a person with "one foot on Earth and one foot in Heaven."

A. *Anxiety*

If this be so, then in addition to our other tensions and worries, we have also this tension between man and God.

This type of tension I call "spiritual anxiety." This is what Augustine was describing when he said, "That soul is restless [anxious] until it finds its rest in God" (*Confessions,* Book I). This spiritual anxiety may be distinguished from other types of anxiety because it concerns itself almost entirely with the problem of meaning of life, rather than with some specific guilt or threat to the ego.

Because the word "anxiety" is widely used today with varying connotations, it is essential that spiritual anxiety be distinguished from other types. Guilt anxiety, for example, is a term widely used in psychiatry. This type of anxiety has two general meanings in psychiatry. One type is the war of the individual with himself. Since man is at war with himself, he often becomes lost in the maze of inner conflicts and so can find no integration, no meaning in his life. That is to say, he wants to be an active and successful person, he tries hard, but the more he tries the more miserably he fails (especially in his own eyes). He therefore feels "guilty." This type of situation Karl Menninger has labeled "Man Against Himself." This set of experiences tends to produce a kind of despair and hopelessness combined with feelings that the person ought not to be this way, that he should do something about it, but he has tried and failed and so stands condemned by his own conscience. Hence, guilt anxiety.

A second type is the war of the individual with society. Guilt anxiety is thus produced by man's relationship to some social group. All of us belong to some group, be it a club, an economic "class," a stratum of society, or some organization. In varying degrees, we see our destiny and purpose in life as rather closely bound up with the destiny of our group. Consciously or unconsciously we tend to assume responsibility both for the group and for ourselves. This is morality. Regardless of our theoretical views about morality, emotionally we operate under the moral code of our group. Right and wrong *do* make a difference to us—an enormous one. We *do* care what our friends think about us; we do tend to follow the moral dictates of our "conscience" (super-ego). Thus, if the group weakens or fails, or if we seem to betray or fail the group, we feel guilty. Pressure is applied either by the group, by our super-ego, or by both and so we feel judged and condemned—guilty. This is the second type of guilt anxiety.

There is another kind of anxiety; namely, neurotic anxiety. This kind usually results from guilt anxiety and is its more severe form. Neurotic anxiety is a serious and intense sense of guilt which results in a flight from life. In this situation, a person has "given up" trying to "atone" for "guilty" deeds, he is weary of fighting himself and life, and so begins to retreat both from inner conflicts and outward social life. He begins to build defenses against social pressures, uses methods of phantasy, illusions—anything to provide escape. Loss of courage takes place; he has no will to fight and win. He becomes "neurotic."

Spiritual anxiety, according to Christianity, differs from all of these types of anxiety. Spiritual anxiety has no particular cause as do the other types. Religious insecurity is more general (though nonetheless real) in origin. The real source of spiritual anxiety is the threat of nothingness. That is to say, most honest people at one time or another become aware of the possibility that life, their life, is utterly meaningless. Any person with integrity faces the general intellectual question of whether life is mad and tragic or not. Such a question becomes personal and emotional in times of stress and conflict. How do we know that life is meaningful? Why should one suffer? For what? Why should we endure the pain and threat of wars and rumors of wars? For what? How do we know that life isn't all "sound and fury signifying nothing"? These are real questions and there is always the real possibility that there isn't any answer to them. Maybe life is meaningless, a nothingness. This, then, is one main source of spiritual anxiety. We are all faced with the threat of nothingness, yet all of us at the same time want to find meaning and purpose in our lives. We are, therefore, in the anxious situation of searching for certainty yet plagued with the threat that such a search is a vain one.

Further, spiritual anxiety is also connected with morality—and here it is also related to guilt anxiety. According to Christian doctrine, some type of moral guilt is both universal and inevitable. That is to say, regardless of the particular morals of any society, *all* human societies will have *some* kind of morals and mores and therefore the individual will always be under some kind of moral pressure, both from society and from the social influences which tend to influence the super-ego. In addition, each individual has his own set of moral values. Thus, Christians say that moral guilt is both universal and inevitable, but *how* one becomes aware of his moral guilt is accidental. This means that in one way or another, every man will have a set of experiences which will tend to make him aware of some moral guilt. I am not here debating which set of moral codes or mores is good or bad. My point is simply that any system or no system, external or internal, provides some kind of moral pressure on man and that sometime he will have an experience of guilt, which in turn will produce guilt anxiety, and which, in turn, increases spiritual anxiety. Thus, the pre-condition of any special act of guilt is the universal sense that we are responsible for at least some parts of our behavior. Spiritual anxiety therefore is partly moral and partly theological. Or, to put it another way, we are spiritually anxious because we know we want to discover some purpose in our lives and because we feel we are responsible for what we do. Yet in both cases we are faced with the possibility that there is no purpose and that we are helpless. This conflict is the domain of spiritual anxiety.

In summary, then, Christian theology maintains that there is the spiritual side of man, that each person is made in the image of God. This image or spirit is constantly seeking its source—God. In terms of behavior and personality structure, it means that we want and must have some attractive meaning and dynamic purpose in our life. But while we know we want it, we seldom find it. Therefore, we are anxious. This is spiritual anxiety—the inner and innate demand in us for meaning, for inner security and peace, for self-fulfillment. This demand or pressure is always present and is perhaps our basic "drive." Since many do not recognize this drive or because they cannot find the fulfillment, they are anxious and restless. It is often spiritual anxiety, which is profound and deep-rooted, that prompts men to sin. Since men cannot stand this anxiety any more than other severe anxieties, they become desperate and seek destructive escapes.

It is just at this point that man's greatest conflict and, therefore, his greatest tension, occurs. To find meaning and power in life—this is man's most profound drive. Yet it is the Christian affirmation that man alone does not possess either the answer or the power. But man always thinks he does! Man always grasps some meaning and some power that is short of God. That is why new discoveries, new enterprises, new programs always attract so many people. We tend to think, "At last, this is it!" And we jump on the band-wagon only to become disillusioned later on when we find that the new movement is not the final answer. The tragic history of many sincere intellectual Communists in the nineteen thirties and their later disillusionment is a case in point. As Christianity sees it, this is the fundamental problem of man: spiritual anxiety which makes man restless. He therefore seeks to escape this tension by finding a powerful answer. It is the Christian faith that man has neither the power nor the meaning within himself or his society. But man always believes he has. And this leads to the Doctrine of Sin. More will be said about the nature of man during and after the discussion of the problem of sin.

5

DOCTRINE OF SIN

THE idea of sin is not a popular one today. It is usually regarded as a hangover from medieval superstition and mumbo-jumbo, or else it is often associated with restrictive "blue laws" and prohibitions against petty vices. In addition, many people reject the doctrine of sin for two other chief reasons: first, because it offends man's pride in all its forms; second, because it is largely misunderstood, and part of this misunderstanding has been caused by certain elements in the church itself. Sin is not sex, drinking, playing cards, smoking or going with those that do. Sin is not necessarily the many so-called "bad deeds," stealing, cheating, graft. Sin is an inner condition of character, an attitude. Specifically defined, sin is the revolt against God. In modern language, sin is the belief that man is self-sufficient, that he is the master of his fate and the captain of his soul. Thus, sin is pride—the pride of man which believes he can save himself from himself (his problems and tensions). The word "pride" should not be confused with pride used in the sense of "snobbishness," or in the sense of respect for achievement. Nor again, should it be identified with the numerous little affections we have for our various abilities or vanities. As it is used here, pride has a much more comprehensive meaning, one which is more akin to the idea of self-sufficiency, or as Webster's dictionary puts it, "inordinate self-esteem."

This comprehensive type of pride is not just a vain whim, but a deep-seated and persistent human attitude which may take several basic forms. There is the pride of the mind or reason, which supposes that man's problems can be solved, life's meaning discovered, and the power to fulfill the meaning achieved by the cultivation of reason. If only men will be rational and objective and use their reason instead of their passions, life's conflicts can be solved. This was the great hope of the Age of Reason, which ended in the age of tyrannical violence.

Then there is the pride of the will—the belief that if a man tries hard enough, wants a thing intensely enough, and applies his will power, he will achieve his end. This is the rugged "go-getter" philosophy. This leads either to tyranny, self-deceit, or frustration. It may lead to tyranny because in man's eagerness to achieve something he may forget other people's wills and try to crush them in order to achieve his own end. It may lead to self-deceit because, when a man gets what he wants, he often finds that that isn't what he really wants. But so much effort has been spent that he does not want to admit to himself the uselessness of his struggle, so he pretends that he is content. Or, lastly, lt leads to frustration for the reason already cited above, and because his aggressiveness mentally clashes with and is limited by other people's wills. Therefore, he is forced to compromise, and is thwarted. The more he is thwarted, the more aggressive he becomes, and so on—another vicious circle.

Then there is also spiritual pride, which is the most subtle and dangerous of all prides. This is the belief that through a certain "religious discipline" or doing of "good deeds" one can become pure and holy and "saved." This is the "bargain theory" of salvation, in which an individual tries to make a bargain with God. He says, in effect, "If I do a certain number of prayers, go to church regularly, and do a certain num-

ber of good deeds each day, then God will make me holy."
This is Phariseeism, and completely ignores Jesus' emphasis
upon inward motive and character. It is the worst kind of
sin because it imagines that sin can be conquered by the
efforts of man. It is dangerous precisely because it is "religious" and invokes the name of God against all opponents.
It is subtle because its motive is essentially a selfish desire
for salvation in the name of unselfish "religious" devotion.

There are many other forms of pride. In general, these
other types can all be grouped under some form of what is
called humanism. Humanism believes that "man is the
measure of all things," that mankind can solve its problems,
is the master of its own destiny. This pride, according to
Christian doctrine, is called sin. This is the fundamental
issue of religion; this is why the Doctrine of Man is so crucial. If it is possible for man by his own powers, abilities,
and resources to solve his conflicts and tensions, and to discover the meaning of life, then, obviously, religion, God,
faith, and Christ are utterly useless. If man is God, then why
bother with any other God? If man has sufficient wisdom and
power to solve life's problems, then why seek wisdom and
power from beyond man? Thus, unless a man believes in the
sin and insufficiency of man, it does no good to talk to him
about Christianity. This is the one crucial issue: "Is, or is
not, man able to save himself?"

It is the Christian faith that man is not able to save himself, and for these reasons: First, it must be recalled that any
given individual has the conflicts and tensions described
above, and that he is the totality of these tensions. To be
sure, a man can always control some of the forces within
himself, but he cannot control all of them or eliminate any
of the fundamental conflicts. Second, an individual person is
finite and cannot, by definition, know all the answers to life.
More important, every person sins in one form or another.

This fact of sin continually compels a man to seek one of the many escapes from tension, in the belief that such an action is not an escape but a real solution to his problems. This attempt also compels a man to put his own interests above those of other men. This prevents a man from being rational and objective. We are all "fair and objective" up to a point. But when the chips are down and it is a question of my money versus yours, or my life against yours, the odds are that you are going to be the loser if I have my way. This sin of inordinate self-interest is the cause of conflict and destruction in life. So long as we have this powerful factor at the very core of our character, neither reason, nor will power, nor ideals, nor economic programs, nor education, will ever solve the problems of conflict. Instead, we will use these instruments primarily in the service of our private desires. Sin, according to Christian doctrine, corrupts these things and perverts them to its own uses. Sin uses reason to rationalize its wants; it uses ideals to hide its real intentions; it manipulates economic policies to suit its needs. A moment's honest reflection should make this clear, for we all do these things. The individual person, then, cannot save himself; he cannot escape from his conflicts and tensions; he has neither the wisdom nor the power.

At long last, most people agree that an individual person cannot pull himself up by his own boot straps. Yet they still retain the belief that mankind as a whole can save mankind. Here, it is asserted, is the solution. While single individuals cannot solve the vast complexities of life, men taken together can. Here the idea is that the bits of wisdom and power that each man possesses can be pooled together for the common good. Thus, you take the best of man and add it all up together and you will have enough to save mankind. This is an enticing and attractive view.

The difficulty, strangely enough, is a very simple one. You

cannot just pluck out and pile up the good qualities of men.
Whether you want to or not, you will also pluck out and
pile up the bad qualities of men. Whenever men get together, whether it be around a peace table, a board meeting, a labor meeting, a committee meeting, a United Nations
meeting, there will be represented not just the good ideas
and intentions of people, but rather the total personalities
involved, the good, the bad, and the indifferent. How could
one possibly carry only "good and true" ideas to any confer-
ence? There is no agreement as to what are "good and true"
ideas anyway. But the self-interests of all are there, too—
in the flesh, in person. At any given period in history one
can accumulate any number of good ideas and good people.
Further, even a superficial look at society should make clear
the truth that individuals are much more rational, moral,
and good than groups of people. One person seldom lynches
another person, but a mob will. One person seldom does
what a nation does. One person seldom dares to say, "myself
right or wrong, but right or wrong, me first." But a collection of persons will not only say but will act on the proposition, "my country right or wrong, but right or wrong, my
country first." Thus it is possible to say in a general way that
relatively speaking, individual man is fairly moral compared
to immoral society.[1] Indeed, the conflicts and tensions of
individual persons are piled exceedingly high in society.
Here the conflicts are the same, but they are much more
obvious, intense, and violent. The good and the bad grow
together and only make the tension between the two forces
greater. Thus, to believe that mankind can save itself, even
though an individual person cannot, seems to contradict the
whole of human history and experience. The truth of the
matter is, from the Christian point of view, neither an

[1] *Cf.* Reinhold Niebuhr, *Moral Man and Immoral Society;* Scribners,
New York, 1932.

individual man nor the whole of mankind can save each other.

Another reason why Christian doctrine holds that man cannot save himself is that man is so built that he seeks God whether he knows it or not, that the facts of experience and history seem to indicate rather clearly that man in his attempt to solve the tensions of existence, inevitably seeks God, either a god or gods. And if he does not find God, or if he denies God, he will create one. He cannot live without one. For the purpose of this point, God will be defined as "that which gives meaning to a man's life," or "that to which man gives allegiance," or "that to which man commits his life." Thus, if a man believes that he can be happy and solve life's problems by the accumulation of money, it may be said that such a man's god is his money. Other people believe that if they can attain power or social prestige, life will be meaningful. Power and social position are thus gods for many people. For others, the state, or some particular economic or political system is god. Still others believe that marriage, or sex, or culture, or business success will bring them happiness and a meaningful life. These ideals to which men commit themselves are gods. People will serve these gods with all degrees of loyalty, even to the point of dying for them. The zeal of the believers demonstrates the religious character of these gods.

So, while some people believe in the Christian God, nearly all others have some kind of a god and believe in it. We are built that way. Human nature is so constructed that we have to have a god. We need desperately something outside ourselves which draws and attracts our energies, something which gives meaning and purpose to our lives, something which we can hope for and trust in. That is why there are really few atheists in the world. Most people who call themselves atheists merely mean that they do not believe in the

God of Christianity. But actually they believe in some other god—the god of self, or reason, or money, or the state. The only true atheist is he who says that life has no meaning whatsoever, all is futile and tragic, man is a stupid, doomed animal in the vast machine of the universe. Some few people assert this, but it is doubtful if they really believe it themselves, or apply it to their own personal existence, because, if this were really true, the only logical thing to do would be to commit suicide. That they do not, betrays the fact that somewhere they think that they are not too stupid and that their own life is just a bit better than tragic, even if they exist only for a few fleeting "pleasures." What is important to note is that man must have a god; he consciously or unconsciously seeks a god. In order to live we must make sense out of life, otherwise we cease to struggle. This is an important point which many young people overlook, mainly because they have not had to face the question directly. But whenever man experiences suffering, pain, and anxiety, he always has to answer the same question, "Why should I endure this?" If a man concludes that life is futile, then his answer to the question is, "I will not endure it. This is too much. Let's end it all." But if he affirms that life does make sense, then the answer is, in effect, "Now I have something to live for. This is worth enduring. In spite of, perhaps because of, this suffering, life makes sense." Thus it can be said that most people, one way or another, do make a decision about the value of life and worship some god which gives them a sense of value and meaning.

The problem arises then as to *which* god shall we follow? This is not the place for a comparative study of the great religions of the world. For the purposes here, it is necessary to distinguish the chief difference between the gods of economics, power, society, self, and the Christian God. The difference is this: When a man's god is a state, or power, or success, such a god is a false one. It is false because such a thing as economic programs or the state is obviously only one thing among others; it is only a particular thing in life—one state among other states, one job among other jobs, one person among other persons. If one "worships" and bets his life on one particular thing in life, one is trying to make it universal. That is, one is assuming that it is the one truth or reality that makes the world go around, that gives meaning to all of life. Some people say, for example, that everything in life can be explained by glands, or by the "economic motive," or by "environment," or by the "self-preservation motive." But as explanations these are obviously too narrow. They explain a lot of things, but not all. No married couple could ever believe or act upon the idea that their love is purely economic or glandular. To say so is to rule out other forces and truths. Thus, when a man's god is any particular thing in life, it is at once limited, narrow, and not wholly true. This is idolatry, which may be defined as taking a particular thing or truth in life and trying to make it universal and all-inclusive. To worship one little facet of truth as if it were the whole truth is to shut one's self off from all other truth and deny that it even exists. In this fashion a little god actually leads to error. This is one reason why idolatry is one of the cardinal sins in the Bible. For idolatry results in putting a puny, false God in the place of the real God. Idolatry is thus a revolt against God by worshipping or trusting a lesser God.

Lastly on this point, if one worships and follows these fake gods, one ends in conflict and despair. They do not solve one's anxieties. If I worship the god of power, my need for love is not satisfied. If I worship and follow the god of the state and that state is defeated in war, my god is defeated. This is why the despair of the Nazis was so great. If my god is success and I do not attain it, my god and my life seem to be futile. And in my struggle to follow one of these gods I will meet other people struggling for other gods. They stand in my way. There is a conflict. All claim their gods are the true ones. Who shall say whether the god of power, or of economics, or of pleasure, or of the state is the one true god and that all others should give way? One particular group has no right to say that its idol is not particular, but universal. If they do, the group and its god often become tyrannical, and that is why so many movements in history become fanatically destructive. They can tolerate no opposition, no criticism. They are right absolutely and completely; therefore, by definition everyone else is wrong and is "impeding the progress of history." False gods, then, are false not only because they are partial, but because they lead us into conflict and destruction, and because history itself defeats them. Again, this is one reason why idolatry is taken so seriously in the Bible. This expression of sin leads to such widespread destruction.

But sin must be brought closer to home. It is so very easy for all of us to talk about sin in general, and perhaps to see its disastrous effects writ large on the world scene. It is also easy to ascribe the sin to somebody else. It is essential, therefore, to emphasize the personal side of sin.

As has been mentioned earlier, personal sin stems from our various anxieties, including spiritual anxiety. Because we do not like this restlessness, we seek to escape it by various means. In psychological terms, it means that all of us have an ego, a picture of ourselves, of what we are and what we would like to be. We want to protect and enlarge this picture—but other people threaten to deface it or destroy it. Therefore, we are anxious about ourselves. Almost everything we do is done with the motive of protecting our ego. I am my chief concern. I tend to be the center of the universe. Though I do not express it as crudely as, "What's in it for me?", that is essentially how I look at life. My greatest love in life is myself. This is what theologians call "inordinate self-love," or sin. This is "undue self-interest." My strongest act of will is to advance myself and my interests. This is why I cannot be completely objective in life; this is why self-interest will tend to corrupt my reason, my "fairness," and my appreciation of others. This is why intelligence and education *per se* are no guarantee of a good and creative character. If I really want something strongly enough, I will use my intelligence and education to get what I want by subtle and clever means. I will persuade, argue, and try to indicate that what I want is good not just for me, but for lots of people. I will say that of course my real motive is service for others and if it should incidentally benefit me, "Why, there's nothing wrong in that." The more intelligent I am, the better chance I have of getting away with selfish aims. My most priceless possession is the picture of myself. And, of course, the view I have is usually a complimentary one! Most often we think more highly of ourselves than we ought to think. Our estimate of ourselves is higher than the facts warrant. One proof of this is the way we resent criticism. We resent it because it might be and probably is right. If we admitted it, we should be forced to lower our opinion of ourselves and perhaps be changed. This hurts our pride; this is a blow to our ego, a threat, a cause for new anxiety, and inspires new resistance to the person challenging us. His criticism offends us; we do not like it; "there's nothing in it for me."

Sin is thus primarily an inward problem of character. Sin concerns the will, motives, attitudes. In defining sin as alienation from God, Christians say that man tends to make himself God. In so doing, man alienates himself not only from the true God but, indeed, from other people. We are so anxious about ourselves that we seek to protect ourselves at all costs and by all means. This is our self-love, our self-interest, our sin. The cause of sin, the source of sin thus lies at the center of human personality. This is most important, for too often people try to understand sin in terms of its *effects,* rather than its *causes.* This has been one of the great mistakes of religious people, who have defined sin in terms of deeds; in this way laws prohibiting certain actions become synonymous with religion. For example, some people have decided that getting drunk—the action itself—is particularly sinful. Therefore, they have made a religio-ethical law which says, in effect, "Thou shalt not drink." From this it seems to follow that alcohol is evil. If a man drinks, he breaks a religious law, is thus a sinner, and is usually condemned. This procedure fails to account for the *motives* of the person who drinks. And in terms of curing this "sinner," the religious legalist does not deal with the real cause of sin; he merely takes away the alcohol. If the legalist succeeds in removing the alcohol, he has not succeeded in removing the man's *desire* for drink. And if the man cannot get drunk, he will turn to something else. It is the old story of trying to solve a problem by dealing with symptoms rather than causes.

The causes of sin always lie within a person; his actions may or may not reflect his inner condition. This is why Christian theology at its best has always been very hesitant about listing actions as sinful. This is why the New Testament emphatically rejects a legalistic system of ethics. For all such systems define sins in terms of deeds with little reference to why people do what they do. One cannot determine whether a man is sinful or not merely by judging what he does. It all depends on his motives, *why* he does certain things. To be sure, there are, in Christianity, sinful actions. For example, murder. But murder is a sin for two reasons: one, because when we kill somebody we are killing a child of God—however bad he may seem to us; two, murder is a sin *if* our motive in killing is a selfish one, such as revenge, hatred, passion for destruction, envy, or jealousy. But what makes this deed a sin is primarily the motive. Therein lies the cause. The murder is the effect. In practical terms, all societies make laws prohibiting murders. We could not exist if murder were "good." And while this law does help restrain some would-be murderers, through the threat of death, it does not prevent all murders, and it does not cure the motives of those who would like to kill somebody but do not dare.

Of course, murder is a fairly clear-cut example. But most of our actions in life are not so clear-cut. Is lying *always* wrong? Sometimes it is not. "White lies," especially in a case where someone is very ill, may be both necessary and right. Fraud and deceit—are they always sinful? Would we not deceive a man who was seeking to violate a woman? Would we tell him where she could be found? People in the underground during World War II had to resort to all kinds of so-called "bad deeds." But were these people sinful because of these actions? These are all highly debatable and the only way a Christian can make a judgment in such matters is to inquire into motives. Thus, some deeds may be sinful because of the motives behind the deed. Similarly, some person may be sinful because he did *not* do some deed. He may have failed to help someone when he could have done so easily. There are sins of omission as well as commission.

Further, a man may be sinful in terms of his thoughts— quite apart from his actions. This point is dramatically recorded in the New Testament. The Pharisees had just found a woman taken in adultery and were roundly condemning her. Jesus restrained them by suggesting that, although the Pharisees hadn't actually indulged in adultery themselves, they probably wanted to and felt like it inside. And so he charged them with the observation that "adultery of the heart" in one sense was just as bad as the deed itself. So from an ultimate point of view, the only difference between the Pharisees and the woman was that the Pharisees were more hypocritical. They wanted to commit adultery, but they didn't dare because of their position. The woman had no position and was obviously insecure, frustrated, and desperate, but at least consistent and honest. Thus, according to Christian doctrine, the real source of sin is in the heart of man, and one cannot make judgments about people unless the *whole* character of the person is known. And when it is known, the judgment, if any, would not be very severe because we would then understand *why* a person did or did not do something. And at the same time, if we were sensitive, we would see that we probably should have done a similar thing under the same circumstances; therefore, humility and tolerance becomes us.

The Christian view of sin is not concerned primarily with a list of bad deeds, but is a description of the basic structure of the personality. Sin is inordinate self-love. I have tried to show some of the many ways in which this "drive" gets us into trouble, why it is essentially destructive rather than constructive. But this immediately brings us to that aspect of man which is most difficult to understand.

According to Christian doctrine, too much self-love is destructive and therefore sinful. On the other hand, it is equally true that too little self-love is also destructive. Some self-love is necessary, in fact it is both good and essential. This point has often been obscured in past history. Emphasis has been placed on the evil in man, and various punishments and disciplines were required to atone for the misdeeds. Sometimes the Church, in attacking excessive optimism, went to the other extreme of excessive pessimism about the worth of man. "Man is totally depraved," or "there is no good in man," or "man must hate himself if he is to love God." These and similar ideas were held by the Church. And while such views can be partly explained and understood by the cultural context in which they occurred, their later effects were not altogether beneficial. For even today, some vestiges of this idea of man's total depravity remain. The idea that man must hate himself if he is really to love God still remains. Many sincere church people over-emphasize the New Testament statement, "Lose your life," and forget the rest of the sentence—"to save (or preserve) your life." The effects of the mystic emphasis on self-abnegation are still with us. Here we are told that we must "empty the self of everything," and create a kind of vacuum so that God can come in. Disciplines of thought, fasting, and physical control are supposed to eliminate the "lusts of the flesh" and the self, so that God can replace the self. But while this practice may have done some good, it is contrary to the spirit of the New Testament and is certainly not the view of man recorded in the teachings of Jesus. The profound wisdom of the Old and New Testament commandment is forgotten: "Thou shalt love the Lord thy God and thy neighbor *as thyself.*" Certainly one of the implications here is that, if we are truly to love God and our neighbor, our devotion to them must be as strong as our love for ourselves. But the command also implies that we cannot really love our neighbor unless we first love ourselves. Further, Jesus' statement that he who would find his life must lose it implies, moreover, that unless a man really loved himself, he would not be willing to endure sacrifices. Indeed, there was considerable pessimism about the worth of man at the time of Jesus. Human lives were cheap then. And certainly a large part of the teachings of Jesus intended to show that men were not cheap, that they had worth and dignity, and that as children of God, they were worth loving. If I am worth the love of my neighbor, I am also worth the love of myself. If somebody thinks that I am worth dying for, then

I owe myself my own love and respect. If, as Christianity says, Jesus died for us that we might know God better, then we cannot be worthless. If He loved us, then why should we hate ourselves? Thus, it seems rather clear to me that in the New Testament there is a genuine insistence on love of self. And certainly this has been verified by modern psychiatry. We know that, if we hate ourselves, we will hate other people. Conversely, only as we love ourselves can we really love other people.

Of course, this attitude must be defined more clearly. It is easy to lift statements about the necessity of self-love out of context and indulge in all kinds of fancies about ourselves. Just as some people have taken the Doctrine of Sin as the whole explanation of man and have ended in a terrible pessimism, so, too, we must beware of insisting on the fact of self-love alone, for then we will become insufferable egotists. Christian doctrine insists on both the idea of sin and the idea of self-love. For in defining healthy self-love, theologians would say that real self-love means respect for self not in spite of imperfections but *because* of imperfections. That is to say, the self is a basic unity of all kinds of forces and attitudes. This basic unity has dignity and worth, or it does not. One cannot split the self into moral boxes, and then love the good ones and hate the bad ones. Indeed, what is it that loves or hates? It is the basic self. Healthy self-love means the ability to live with our own limitations, quirks, and neurotic tendencies without smugness or despair. This is perhaps difficult to define in words. But consider the alternatives. If we love ourselves only on the condition that we are near-perfect, since we are imperfect, we cannot love ourselves. If we wait until we have no faults and limitations, we will wait forever and will be most unhappy and uncreative. If we imagine ourselves to be perfect (or nearly so), we will be impossible to live with and will destroy ourselves by our fantastic illusion of greatness.

On the other hand, if loving ourselves meant complete satisfaction with our personality structure, behavior, and ideas, then we would stop growing and also be very difficult to live with. Many of us, indeed, do just this. We have been told so often that we are merely products of our environment and/or inner drives and early environment, that we tend to believe we can do nothing to change ourselves. "I am what I am!" This leads to stagnation and sterility as well as to smugness and conceit. We can excuse anything we do or not do by declaring our helplessness. And thereby we cease to grow and mature. Exclusive emphasis on either determinism or innate sin destroys genuine self-love, and hampers creative love of both self and neighbor. Thus, Christian theology states that creative self-love includes awareness of man's sinful character, and also man's God-given, creative character. Healthy self-love means a realistic appraisal of ourselves as we really are in our totality, and above all it means that as a mixture of good and evil, we are of worth and dignity. We do not love only the good in ourselves or other people and hate the evil. We love the *total person—as he is*—or we do not love him at all. We love ourselves—in our totality—or we do not love ourselves at all. It is the height of arrogance to say that we love the good qualities of our wife, but hate the bad. One loves all of his mate—the totality of the "good, bad and indifferent"—or not at all. The real test of love, therefore, is how well it accepts the facts of imperfection and corruption and yet remains strong and creative.

Thus, the Christian Doctrine of Man is neither a sombre judgment that man is merely a groveling, selfish animal worth nothing, nor is it a facile description of man as a saintly cherub who can hardly wait to do good to all men. To contemporary secularists, Christian theology has emphasized the Doctrine of Sin because theologians believe that the secularists do not always understand the depths to which human beings can sink or because secularists attribute destructive behavior to fairly simple causes such as poverty, culture, or the Oedipus complex. On the other hand, to many contemporary religionists, Christians also have to emphasize the dignity of man because these religionists tend to belittle man to the point where he is rendered helpless. They substitute a divine determinism for a naturalistic one. In either case, it seems to me that a rigid determinism, be it naturalistic or divine, tends to destroy both the personality and meaning to life.

The conclusion, then, is that man is both a sinner and a saint, creative and destructive, a bundle of tensions, and that he is both good and bad but he is also redeemable. The Christian view of man is therefore neither optimistic nor pessimistic. Christian faith holds that man cannot save himself from himself by himself. But it asserts that man *can be* saved by God. How this is effected will be described later in the chapter on conversion. The important point here is the Christian doctrine of man in his "natural condition." For again, this is the crucial doctrine. If man is so built that he can solve his own anxieties, loves, and hates, then there is no need of religion and God. On the other hand, if man cannot solve his own problems, then religion becomes essential. Yet one does not argue a person into either conclusion. One has to take the Christian insights and descriptions and see how nearly they jibe with empirical facts, and, especially, whether they provide meaningful interpretations of our own private and social experiences. It is the Christian faith, of course, that this view of man is fortified with abundant empirical data and provides people with the most meaningful understanding of themselves and the world in which they live.

6

DOCTRINE OF GOD

BEFORE the Christian Doctrine of God is stated, some of the problems involved in any discussion of God must be mentioned again. This is necessary because many of us have had, or think we have had, no experience of God. The word "God" seems to remain just a word, or perhaps it suggests the childish idea of a divine Santa Claus, or just "an oblong blur." Therefore, when some minister discusses God, his whole talk may be fruitless. We simply may not know what he means. One of our problems, therefore, is to state the problem of God!

The problem, as I see it, is this: All the world's great religions, philosophies, and sciences represent, in their own ways and by their own different methods, the search for the basic reality which makes the world go around. The problem for all of us is, "What is the most real thing or power in life?" The natural scientist wants to find out what is the most basic and determining stuff or power behind natural life in all of its manifestations. The philosopher wants to find out if there is any uniting principle of truth by which one can understand all the various little truths which are available. The religionist wants to find out if there is a reality or power which lies behind both nature and truth and life itself—what this reality is like. This search by mankind is not motivated by mere curiosity, nor is it an endeavor limited only to a few scholars. The basic drive behind most people is the need of finding meaning to life.

We seem to be so built that we are never satisfied with things as they are. The scientist is not content with observing phenomena; he wants to know causes, and to see if he can discover some intelligible pattern in natural events. He wants to be able to predict future events on the basis of his knowledge of past order. The philosopher is not content to record different ideas; he wants to find some common principle of truth which can unite and relate the various opinions and concepts. The religionist is not content with his own private religious experience; he wants to find out the common basic reality behind all experience, and see if perhaps different religious ideas can be resolved more harmoniously. The point here is that, whether the search is conducted on a highly intellectual basis or on the common level of "making sense out of life," all men are trying to do the same thing. We all have thousands of differing experiences, opinions, attitudes, prides, and prejudices. We have hundreds of daily problems —personal, social, political, and psychological. We have joys and fears, tragedies and triumphs. But how to organize all these experiences into a unified and intelligible order? As was suggested earlier, when man is faced with tragedy and suffering, the question becomes intense: Why should I endure pain and anxiety? Is life (my life) worth-while? Is there meaning to it? We may not ask these questions in so many words, but we *feel* them. And our decision, articulate or not, usually answers that there is some sense to life in spite of its complexities and contradictions. I am suggesting, then, that all people have to discover some meaning in life in order to live it. And the meaning that is given to life usually involves some idea that there is a basic reality behind all other realities, and that this basic reality, which is the most important thing in life, is worthy of one's trust and devotion. It is *the* thing or power by which one determines his life or allows it to be determined.

This basic reality may be defined in many ways. For some people, the self is their basic loyalty. For others, it may be the family; still others, the state, or some "program." For others, it may be nature, or many gods as in ancient primitive religions. But whatever the labels or objects, everyone has something which seems to him to be the most powerful and meaningful reality in life and he orders his life according to that meaning. In the broadest sense, then, this is what is meant by the word God. That is why religion may be defined as "the affirmation that life has meaning." God, or gods, may be defined as "that which gives meaning to life" or "the determiner of one's destiny."

Conversely, genuine atheism is the denial that life has meaning or sense. That is why there are very few real atheists in life. Not many people seriously believe that life, especially their own, is meaningless and unworthy. Most people who say that they are atheists mean that they do not believe in some particular definition of a god. Many sincere people who think that Christianity defines God as some kind of benevolent tyrant do not believe in this kind of God and therefore say that they are atheists. Actually, these same people usually have found a very real meaning in their lives. Their "determiner of destiny" may well be a firm belief in the orderliness of nature and devotion to great principles of freedom and moral advance for mankind. Such people are not atheists as we have defined the term. They find life intensely worth-while and meaningful. They believe with great conviction that there is some kind of basic order and reality in nature and human life. Their God may not be one of the gods defined by religionists, but their god is every bit as real to them, and their devotion to it every bit as strong as anybody else's faith and service.

The "problem of God" is partly semantic. The problem also includes the attempt to discover whether there is some basic or ultimate reality behind all other appearance, some primal power which gives life its source, direction, and order. And further, if there is such a reality, it is essential to discover how we can know it and what it is like. The word "God" is, by common agreement, the label used to designate Ultimate Reality, basic power, "that which makes the world go around." God, or gods, are words which point to what people regard as the foundation of their meaning to life. It will help a great deal in our understanding if we begin to us the label God in this sense, and eliminate crude and naive images of God.

It is essential to note here that there is no one complete definition of God. God cannot be contained in one human definition. This is not to say that all definitions or descriptions of God are equally true. It is to emphasize that no single explanation, nor all definitions taken together can reveal the full nature of God. Theology, like all other enterprises in life, is limited and limited even in its own field. All doctrinal statements, creeds, and dogmas are made by human beings, however saintly, however much the Holy Spirit may be operating through them. In short, *there is no final and complete description of Ultimate Reality—God.*

Thus far, we have defined God as Ultimate Reality, the basic power behind life, the "Determiner of Destiny." These are all abstract ideas and can have a variety of interpretations. And they are so broad as to be almost meaningless as they stand. Therefore, the next question might well be, "What do you mean by Ultimate Reality?" The Christian answer might be described in this fashion.

First of all, in the New Testament, Jesus' most frequent description of God was "Father." God is like a father. But what is a father like?

The word as used in Jesus' time meant something quite different than present-day usage. Today, father means to many the nice, hard-working fellow who is not seen very often but who can be counted on for that inevitable twenty-five dollar "loan" for houseparty week-end. Or, to others he is still the hard-working fellow but one who is also somewhat overshadowed by his attractive and sometimes dominating wife. Today, mother is often God to the children. Yesterday, father was God to the children.

In Jesus' time it was definitely a man's world. The father in those days was the absolute power in the household. He was the patriarch who dispensed love and justice. Indeed, the father sometimes had the power of life and death over his children and his wife. Thus, as Jesus used the term, father meant the symbol of love and justice. The father was a righteous and just man who stood for, and maintained justice without fear or favor. But this justice and righteous rule were enforced not in spite of but because of his love for his children. "The Lord chasteneth whom he loveth" in the interests of correcting his children. Even today, parents have to deal justly with their children, scolding them with affection, not because they hate their children, but because they want to guide them to responsible maturity. Thus, when Jesus used the word Father, His hearers understood at least two main aspects of God's nature: that God is both just and loving.

To translate these concepts in modern terms, it may be said that ultimate reality is not blind fate, but is a power which guarantees order, both natural and moral, and at the same time is concerned with human beings. This means that the structure of life has some order; most of nature and human nature live in accordance with orderly laws. Things do not happen in disorderly fashion. The sun will not come up in the east one day and then rise in the west the next day. Also, if God is a power which contains elements of justice and righteousness, then this means that life is so built, history is so ordered that goodness will win out ultimately, and that the power of the universe is on the side of righteousness. This is the Christian view of God as the author and sustainer of goodness in life.

Further, God as Father meant, to Jesus' listeners, the idea that ultimate reality was purposive. Indeed, this was not a new idea at all, for it was assumed throughout the Old Testament. If God is power and is the source and sustainer of creativity and justice, then obviously there is a purpose behind everything. This is what is meant when it is said that Reality or God is not blind. There is a "grand design" to the universe; the order in it is there for some reason. History moves along according to some moral purpose. Nature seems to be an orderly process, but process for what? For some high purpose. Just exactly what this purpose is has not been divined by man yet. Perhaps we will never know exactly and completely the purpose of everything. But both Judaism and Christianity believe intensely that the power of God, the whole process of life is purposive.

Some definitions or explanations of this purpose can be given. For instance, one can say that the basic purpose of human life is to love and serve God. In so doing, one achieves genuine happiness and creativity which gives life an eternal or lasting quality. It is said that the process of nature seems to be approaching some great perfection, that as man grows in stature, so nature grows, that, if man abides by and cooperates with the "laws of nature," man will benefit by the vast resources of power and matter in nature. More than that, if man abides by and cooperates with "spiritual laws," he will benefit by achieving more maturity, creative power, and greater moral wisdom with which he can use nature's powers for better ends. For without spiritual power, man tends to exploit and violate nature to his own detriment. There seems to be a unity of cooperating purpose, therefore, between

God, Man and Nature, and all three must be in harmony. If not, destruction is let loose.

But there are further questions one could ask about "the purpose of life." If this purpose is as described above, why is it that way and not some other way? The answer to that is very simple: We do not know. Similarly, if we ask why a tree is made the way it is instead of some other way, we have to say we do not know. But the hardest questions about God's purposes usually appear in detail. And most of these center on the problem of suffering and evil which will be taken up later. Yet it must be said here that most of the questions asked about purpose cannot be answered completely, and few of them even satisfactorily. The idea of purpose in nature, history, and the whole process of life is essentially derived from one's whole concept and experience of God. The idea of purpose fits quite clearly and logically into the whole pattern of the description of God. If God is like a father, then it would be illogical to regard a father as having no purpose in bringing up his children. One can point to some "evidences" of purpose in life, but it is quite true that one cannot set out with a blank mind and discover "purpose" in life. The belief in purpose in life stems primarily from one's faith in God, and though it is supported by some credible evidences, it cannot be proved by these evidences. So, Christian theologians believe that the life process is purposive and describe that purpose in a general way. One of the functions and problems of theology is to detect and describe just how that purpose operates in detail and what it means for us in our daily living.

Thus far in the description of God, I have used the word father as I believe Jesus used it. And it should be pointed out that the descriptions used by Jesus were all in the Old Testament tradition. For this reason, the listeners of Jesus did not need to have all this explained. From their religious heritage, they knew already what the symbol "Father" meant. The Old Testament religion emphasized again and again that God was the creating and sustaining power of the universe, that He was "The Lord of History," that He was a moral god who was the source and ground of justice and righteousness, that, therefore, the life process was purposive and meaningful.

Because evolution has become a growing, scientific concept, many people are still bothered by the apparent conflict between the idea of a Creator God and that of the scientific account of evolution. Though this problem reached sensational and tragic proportions a century ago, it is still a very real problem for many today.

Much of the difficulty is due, in my opinion, to the confusion between the functions of science and religion. From what was said earlier in this book about the nature of the two enterprises, it should be recalled that there is no necessary dispute between them. To the problem of evolution, religion and science can be applied in this manner. Science describes *how* and *when* the universe and life began. Religion seeks to discover *why* life started.

If the accounts in Genesis are regarded as attempts at scientific description of creation, it is quite true that such accounts are in sharp conflict with those of modern science. On the other hand, if the stories in Genesis are viewed as endeavors to explain the religious views of the Hebrews, then the conflict need not arise. What were these religious beliefs? The writers of Genesis were trying to say that life was purposeful and moral. If God was good, then what he created must be good. "And God saw that *it was* good" (Genesis 1:12).

There is no doubt, on the other hand, that many religious folk have regarded the biblical story as a scientific account. It may well be that the authors of Genesis believed this too. Since there were no scientific descriptions at that time, it is understandable why men did accept such a view. Today, however, contemporary Christian theologians are aware of the problem. Their answer is this: Scientific data and theories on evolution must be accepted. But when this is done, the age-old religious questions still remain. Is the process of evolution purposeful? Why was human life created? Who or what was the primary source? These theological questions cannot be answered by science.

There are at least two ways by which theologians try to answer such questions. One method is to use formal logic. Another method is to use symbolic stories and myths. This latter way purposely utilizes current fables and popular symbols and re-interprets them in order to emphasize one main idea. There is considerable evidence that the authors of Genesis may have used this method. It is quite clear that they borrowed the creation story from earlier writers in other religions. Whether the Old Testament writers believed these stories to be factually true is open to debate. But it is certainly obvious that they adapted and re-interpreted the stories to suit their purposes.

Contemporary Christian theologians, then, regard the accounts in Genesis as false scientifically, but extremely useful in suggesting answers to the religious questions. The myth of Adam and Eve, for example, is called a myth because it is not true from a biological point of view. What the myth conveys in a religious sense is profoundly true. The myth suggests that one of the basic causes of evil in human affairs is man's pride which prompts him to believe that he can obtain perfect knowledge.

In summary, then, the Bible must not be regarded as a scientific treatise. To do so, is to misunderstand it and to neglect its many profound religious insights.

Let us return to our description of God as Father. There is another side to God's nature—the personal. Because people were already familiar with the impersonal meanings of God as Father, Jesus emphasized the intimately personal aspect of the father-child relationship. And here, first of all, was the idea of God as Love. Of course, the Old Testament, especially the prophet Hosea, saw God as a god of love, but Jesus emphasized the point again and carried the implications further. Though the ancient Hebrew father may have been stern and just, he was also tender in his affections towards his children. His love was his dominant motive even if we think he expressed that love harshly. The point, however, is that love was central. The father loved his children with great intensity. It is no accident that even today the Jews illustrate the highest degree of family devotion of any peoples.

So it was that Jesus could make crystal clear that God was not only a power, but that He was Love, a power that cared. God is the Father, all men are his children. The relationship between reality and man, therefore, is not one of indifference, nor slavish obedience, but one of loving response. The impersonal attributes of creative power, moral and natural order, are part of the activity of God, but they are also intimately associated with God's love. In a very real sense, one might even say that they are expressions of love because they make human and natural life possible and help determine its character just as human parents provide a structure and order of existence for their children.

Jesus also suggested *how* God's love operates when he used the symbol Father. And when he described how the love operates, he also defined the nature of this love. It should be noted, for example, that God's love is not sentimental, as is some human love. God's love is not the kind that overlooks evil and destruction. God is not going to spoil His children by letting them "get away with murder," nor, on the other hand, is He going to tyrannize over them and force them against their wills to become saints. The essence of God's love is spontaneity and freedom. God freely loves all men—good, bad and indifferent. As will be explained later, "For God so loved the world, that He gave His only begotten Son, that whosoever believeth in him should not perish, but have everlasting life" (John 3:16). What is expected in return is the free response of man. But if man does not respond to this offer of love, there will be no death-dealing thunderbolts and lightning, no plague to scare him into loving God. God will continue to love and seek man out.

On the other hand, He will not let man engage in wanton behavior and destruction without limit. If man persists in this course, His law of life is so built that serenity disappears and happiness is reduced. This does not mean that God "picks on" individuals with capricious malice. It means that there is a limit to man's freedom, a limit which prevents chaos. If a man is foolish enough to scoff at the law of gravity and jumps out of a second story window in order to prove that there isn't any such law, we know what will happen. If he is lucky, he may survive with two broken legs. It would be childish to say that Nature broke the man's legs. It would be much more mature to say that the man's foolishness or ignorance resulted in the fractures. Similarly, with God's activity, we do not say that God out of meanness makes a man unhappy or sick. We say that man's ignorance or pride led to his difficulty. Thus, God loves man and wishes man to love Him in return. But if man does not respond, then man will not find his maximum creativity and happiness. Even so, God still loves wayward man.

This suggests another quality of God's love; namely, its sacrificial nature. God's love gives without regard to returns. It is not dependent upon rewards or responses, it is freely given without favor or merits. It asks nothing in return and remains constant throughout. This is one of the real tests of love—to be able to love even though the object of your love denies you. This is what is called divine love; divine because so far as we can observe in human nature, only God is capable of perfectly loving in this way. Probably all human beings in varying degrees must have some return, some response, in order to keep on loving. Human love tends to be mutual love —we will love if somebody gives us something in return. Divine love is sacrificial love; it will love regardless—even in the face of arrogant and bitter denial. And the theological term "Grace" really means this aspect of divine love; that is, God's love is given to us freely, even though we do not deserve it, or more radically, even though we do not want it. God's love, therefore, is equated with Perfection—the standard by which is measured all other expressions of love.

When Jesus emphasized this type of love, He was giving a new definition of God's love. In the past, God's love was thought to be dependent upon man's moral achievements. Most primitive religions, including some types of Judaism, held that if man obeyed certain laws and commandments, if he achieved some moral or religious status, then God, as a reward, would love man. Conversely, if man did not succeed in fulfilling the requirements, God would punish man. Jesus broke away from these covenantal ideas by saying that God's love is not dependent upon anything that man does or does not do. God's love is always available to man regardless of what man is or does.

Moreover, since God is love and the source of goodness, man cannot be "religious" or moral unless God is operating in and through man in the first place. Christianity would say that man becomes moral and religious only as he is the vehicle of God's love. We do not first become morally good and religiously pure and then find God. If that were true, one might well raise the question of why God at all? If we, as men, can be morally strong and religiously (spiritually) mature by our own efforts, then what need is there for a God except perhaps as a kind of spiritual lollipop reward for having achieved our goal? Thus, Jesus is saying that God is love, a freely-giving, sacrificial love available to all men.

This concept of sacrificial love may sound abstract and mysterious, but if we consider evidences or analogies even on the human level, it should be more real to us. Imagine a human parent telling his child that if the child did anything wrong or mischievous, the father would stop loving the child. Suppose a parent said that she would hate her child when he did wrong, and love him dearly when he did right? The child would soon be a hopeless neurotic. Even on our human level, most wise parents love their children freely regardless of whether the children do "good" or "bad." So, too, with "Our Father in Heaven."

There is another reason why Jesus stressed the personal characteristic of God, and that is because of the problem of knowing God. If God—Ultimate Reality—were only a vague, impersonal power, or were only an abstract idea, much like the First Cause, we might be able to accept these as intellectual concepts. But if God was only a series of abstract concepts, it is fair to say that God would have little relevance to our lives, and provide us with almost no real meaning and understanding about life. I suspect that for many people the real reason why God is not a power in their lives is because their knowledge and acquaintance with God is almost entirely intellectual. It is perhaps significant that Greece, in the period of the philosophers, described God in terms of abstract ideas or First Principles, whereas Israel, in the time of the great prophets, described God as a righteous person. This is not to say that either the Greeks or Hebrews were totally wrong or right. It is simply to point out that in addition to intellectual problems, the experiential problem is important, too.

Part of God's nature must be known and understood

through the mind; God is impersonal in the sense of creative power; God is, Christians believe, rational rather than irrational; God's power is operative within His intelligence or Purpose. He may be the Prime Mover, the First Cause, the Divine Mind of the Universe. The point is not to stop with those definitions. So, *in addition,* Christians say that God is personal. By this is meant essentially that He can be experienced. If God is love (and we have not yet "proved" that He is), then God must be known by man through experience. Love as an abstract idea is fairly meaningless and powerless. But love experienced is something very potent and meaningful. Therefore, when Jesus described God as love He was certainly, among other things, emphasizing the personal side of God.

It is this aspect of God which has caused so much confusion in the history of religious thought and practical religion. In all ages, particularly our own, the idea that God is personal has offended many people. And there has been considerable justification for this offense. For many religionists, in trying to make God real and concrete, have gone too far. Consequently, God has been pictured in all-too-human terms (anthropomorphism is the official label). It is quite true that God has often been described as a severe, harsh judge or tyrant, or, on the other hand, as a kindly, sweet, loving person with very little power—a kind of good but helpless power or figure. And some otherwise adult people retain childish conceptions of God as a benevolent man with a beard who lives just out of sight above the clouds. Now, of course, if these pictures of God are taken literally and as the whole story about God, no intelligent person could believe in God. When most moderns say that they do not believe in a personal God they usually mean that they do not believe in one of these childish descriptions of God. And Christians would agree entirely. When Christian theologians use the word "personal" in their definition of God, they are merely trying to say that God can be experienced personally by man. God is personal in the sense that love is personal. God is like a father and therefore can be known by His children; God is love and therefore, like love, can be known and experienced.

I have stressed this personal side of God, as it is emphasized in the New Testament, in an attempt to make God more real —at least to our understanding. But we still have far to go. As we went along in the descriptions, we found ourselves using terms which often seem contradictory. For example, we used the two words, personal and impersonal. Strictly speaking and at first glance, we might conclude that these two words are contradictory. We might be tempted to say that a person cannot be personal and impersonal at the same time in his relationship with another person. The fact is, however, that all of us do illustrate precisely the point that we can and are personal and impersonal most of the time. We say we treat our employees impersonally—meaning we do not play favorites. Yet we also say that we treat them personally—meaning we care about them and their welfare. Yet in the field of religion, a controversy still rages over this problem. In almost every age somebody is debating whether God is personal or impersonal. Similarly, with other characteristics: Is God righteous or loving? Is God a god of justice or mercy? Does God work in history or is He beyond history? People have taken one side as over against the other, epithets have been hurled at each other, labels pinned, people persecuted and condemned and excommunicated, and what all. The tragedy is that most of this was unnecessary.

For Christian theology at its best has insisted that all of these are false questions, false alternatives. They are akin to the old legal trick question, "Answer yes or no: do you still beat your wife?" They are like questions which ask, "Do you laugh or cry?" "Are you good or bad?" "Are you brave or afraid?" From the Christian point of view, the answer to most of these questions is "yes and no" or "both." Christianity, therefore, would maintain that God is both personal and impersonal, righteous and loving, just and merciful, that He operates in history, but is also beyond history. Theologians do not see that these are contradictions at all. For even on the human level, it seems quite clear that most human beings are righteous and loving at times, that parents remind their children of the demands of justice but are also merciful and forgiving, and that persons live in society and yet retain some small private bastion of individuality. I see no contradictions, therefore, in the terms used to describe the nature of God. Again, however, it must be emphasized that in defining God, Christian theologians would insist that we do not cling to one set of terms or words. The more concepts we can use to describe the essential mystery of life, the more adequate and more nearly complete will be our knowledge and understanding of God. With this warning in mind, let us turn to one of the classical Christian definitions of God.

The historic description is called the "Trinitarian Formula"—God as Father, Son and Holy Spirit (Ghost). The idea of God as Father has already been elaborated. The concept of God as Son is used to describe God's activity in revealing Himself to mankind through Jesus. Since this is the most central doctrine in Christianity, it will be discussed fully in a separate chapter—the Doctrine of Christ.

The Doctrine of God as Holy Spirit is used to describe both the personal side of God and His present activity. This doctrine is another tenet which has caused much disagreement and confusion. Originally, in Christian theology, the Holy Spirit meant that God worked in a special way within the fellowship of the Church. As a matter of experience in the early Church, it was quite apparent that the apostles, devoted servants, and followers displayed unusual zeal and vigor. If the New Testament record in the Book of Acts and the Epistles of Paul is reasonably accurate, not only did the early Christians show intense devotion but they also did some unusual things. Though today we might not regard their many types of faith healing as miracles, in those days such events were regarded as at least minor miracles. But even apart from these happenings, there is no doubt that the early Christians, in spite of some of their quarrels, had a very high degree of unanimity, intense loyalty to Christ, and a passionate commitment to His cause which led them even into martyrdom. For this reason, one of the descriptions used to explain this fervent activity was the idea of the Holy Spirit. Certainly there was a special spirit in this early group of Christians; a spirit, a motivation, a comradeship unlike that of any other group. The early Christians all had a very real sense of the living Christ, an intense awareness of the presence of God in their own experience. They could not explain it away by merely saying they were "enthusiastic" about a particular social phenomenon. To them, it was the most real thing in their lives; it surpassed ordinary human intensity or depth. For them, the content of their feelings seemed to be divine. Nothing less could characterize their spiritual experience. God was not a far-off principle, a First Cause, or only an impersonal Power. God was active, personal, here and now, operating in and through them—a living Power. The Holy Spirit, then, meant that God was acting in a special way within this group, in a way that was unique. The Doctrine of the Holy Spirit is, therefore, the idea that God operates in a special way in the Church—in the community of believers in Christ. This was the original doctrine.

Today, many sincere Christians do not agree with this interpretation. One of the modern views of the Holy Spirit is the idea that the Holy Spirit is not limited to the community of believers in Christ (the Church), but is in everybody, in all men—or nearly all. And another modern view is that the Holy Spirit is not only in all humans, but in nature as well. Holy Spirit here means simply the presence or activity of God everywhere in life. It is not the purpose here to argue the many possible interpretations. The point is to explain the original and orthodox Doctrine of the Holy Spirit. And this is not to say that the modern views are all wrong because they are modern. While I personally believe there are certain dangers and confusions involved in some recent interpretations, most of them contain the original idea but go on to expand it. And the orthodox view in later history tended to become too narrow and at times was asserted as *"the* test" of being a Christian. Taken as but one of many descriptions of the nature of God, I believe it to be true. It does not seem to me to be too narrow or fatuous to hold to the original view of the Holy Spirit. For even in ordinary secular groups there seems to be a fair analogy. A highly integrated group of people, sharing common convictions and purposes, display a group spirit which is unique to that group. We say, for example, that a football team has "spirit," or we speak of the American "temper," German "Kultur," and Russian "ethos." When we do this we are describing an empirical event; namely, that a particular group has some power which motivates them to great heights of energy and devotion. Each group has a "spirit" or character of its own. One group has a martial spirit, another has an idealistic spirit, another a crusading spirit, still another, a quiet, serene spirit, and so on. The early Church, similarly, had a spirit of its own. It certainly had all the spirit of any other social group, but in addition, its members felt that there was something more—the spirit of God, the Holy Spirit.

Moreover, it has been the experience of millions of Christians since that they have felt and known the living God through the Church. Most Christians became Christians by their membership and activity in a community of believers —a Church. Few people, if any, have discovered the Christian God in isolation. This is one doctrine which is supported by a great deal of empirical evidence. It is not "proved" by the personal experience of millions of Christians, but the testimony of so many people certainly lends a large mass of creditable support. But it is necessary to stress again that in maintaining this doctrine, it is not done so exclusively. In asserting belief in the validity of the Holy Spirit as described above, I am *not* saying that God acts *only* in this way. I am not saying that other people cannot know a great deal about the nature of God in other ways. Indeed, theologians emphatically agree that God is known in a thousand different ways, that "He left not himself without witness" among all lands and peoples (Acts 14:17). This interpretation of the Doctrine of the Holy Spirit is merely saying that in addition to whatever other ways God can be experienced, He can *also* be experienced in this special way. "For where two or three are gathered together in my name, there am I in the midst of them" (Matthew 18:20). This is the biblical statement which most clearly suggests what is meant by the Holy Spirit.

Thus, the Trinitarian Formula is another attempt to describe the nature of God. Historically, it has been the most popular and the most helpful. Like all good things, it has been used and misused, explained away too broadly at times, narrowed down too exclusively at other times. But throughout Christian history it has remained the standard definition of God. Yet it still causes many moderns much difficulty. Some feel that it makes God into three gods—a polytheism. Some feel that it is too narrow, or that it is rationally absurd. Most of these objections stem, I believe, from either a misreading of the doctrine or a too literal understanding of the concepts. If one regards each of the three parts as describing the whole nature of God, then one might well conclude that Christianity has three complete Gods. But if one regards each part of the Formula and the whole together as still only a limited and incomplete description of God, then it seems to me the polytheistic conclusion can be avoided.

One of the historic Christian replies to this problem is the statement, "One God in three aspects." And we might add or re-interpret, "One God in three of His many aspects." The nearest analogy I can think of is that of a child discovering electricity.

"What is electricity, Daddy?"

"Well, son, electricity is a power that does many things, or acts in different ways—like that light bulb there. See, it makes light." The son nods understandingly, but then leans on the hot electric stove, slightly burning his hand.

"What's that, Daddy?" he asks.

"That's electricity, too—used as heat." A few moments later, the son is playing near the floor plug and gets a little shock.

"What's *that,* Daddy?" he asks again—somewhat irritated, if not hurt.

Again, Daddy replies, "Well, son, that's electricity, too."

"But you said the light bulb was electricity. Then you said the stove was, and now you say the plug is electricity. Why don't you make up your mind which is which?"

"I know, son, it does seem as if I have given three different answers, but if you remember at the beginning I said that electricity is a kind of power or energy that acts or is used in many different ways. Here in our house we have seen and you have felt how it is used in three ways. But it is the same power operating in three different aspects."

If the above conversation were in a Hollywood movie, it would then conclude with:

> "Oh, I see, Daddy. That makes it all perfectly clear to me. Thank you."

And the child would then go on with his blocks to build a hydro-electric station and Daddy would sit down with his newspaper beaming with pride at his own ability at lucid explanation and satisfaction with his son's unusual intelligence. Since we are not recording this from a movie, the average father and child would probably continue with many other questions and neither would be satisfied that the other understood what was said, but both would have learned something and their relationship enriched. At any rate, the analogy, I believe, is a fair one in that it suggests that any non-material entity, energy, or power, usually has to be explained in several ways according to its various manifestations.

So, in the Trinitarian Formula, the attempt is made to show at least three chief ways in which God's power can be seen or understood. To take any one of the three aspects and try and pit it against the other leads to absurdity just as it would in the case of electric power. The statements made sense as a unity, or not at all. But whether one can make sense out of the whole explanation or not is another problem which again is not "proved" merely by evidences or pure logic, but is a problem for faith together with the evidences. Yet it is our firm conviction that any genuine understanding of God will require many definitions of what we mean by "God" and our problem is to acquire a set of explanations which, though varied, are internally consistent and comprehensive. God cannot be confined in one human definition. Therefore, many descriptions are necessary. But not all descriptions are equally good. There must be some cohesive logic in them. Christian theologians would not, for example, say that it is perfectly valid for a person to believe that God is a sadistic tyrant who enjoys making people suffer, and then also believe that God is a loving power who seeks to redeem people and help them live more abundantly. Similarly, if a person said that he was tolerant, comprehensive, and broad-minded because he held that $2 + 2 = 4$ and it also may equal 5, the verdict would be that such was nonsense. But if he said that the two numbers (2) are not limited to making the sum 4, but could be used in several ways, either subtracted to make zero, or put together to make 22, then he does make sense. But they cannot be used just any old way; $2 + 2$ can never make 23 or 7 or 113. Just any old definition of God will not do, either. It must have some relation to the experiences of man, some logical consistency, some coherence with other definitions of God.

Thus, Christianity has a set of definitions and descriptions of God which it believes have been derived partly from the experiences of many people, partly from our rational attempts to make them consistent and communicable, partly from insights of faith, and partly corroborated by the experiences and minds of thousands of other Christians. For these reasons, among others, Christians believe that they know something about God, about the Ultimate Reality of the Universe. They believe enough is known to make sense out of life, enough to make a tremendous difference in the way life can be lived. But Christians also know they do not know everything, that there is still, and always will be, much about God they do not experience or understand. One of the problems and responsibilities of all Christians, clergy and laymen alike, is to make more clear and more real both to ourselves and to others the nature of God and how He operates.

The problem of unity of belief and agreement on the nature of God is not as simple as many tend to think, nor as impossible as some people claim. With respect to differences of opinion, this much can be said: The bitter controversies and persecutions in all histories of religions has been due largely to the insistence of those in power on conformity to narrow doctrines, and the claim that one or two of these doctrines is *the* one and complete or only definition of God. And while I believe such a position to be false and a subversion of the New Testament spirit, it must also be said that the opponents in many instances were guilty of the same error. They wished to substitute some other narrow set of definitions with the claim that *they* were the exhaustive and final descriptions of God. In such cases, my judgment would be directed against both parties. For regardless of who did win, or who might have won, the results would have been the same—tyranny of a particular dogma followed by bitter persecution.

On the other hand, some of the controversies were on a higher level than this, for another problem of diversity is that of "watering down the faith." It was mentioned above that Christian theologians believe in the necessity of many descriptions of God, but that not all these explanations are acceptable. This raises the problem of how one decides what is acceptable and what is not acceptable, and who does the deciding. Thus, in the history of Christian thought, some of the controversies were on this very problem. When Christianity became the popular religion of the Roman world, it was not long before people were combining all sorts of beliefs, rituals and practices and calling them the Christian Faith. Ancient mystery cults, primitive ethical practices, various philosophical views, and nationalistic mores, were all covered with a facade of Christianity. Everybody was doing all kinds of strange and contradictory things, yet everybody was claiming that "this" was Christianity. The situation then was much like certain problems today. For example, everybody claims he's "for freedom." Yet America and Russia differ radically in their view of what freedom means and what it entails in practice, but both claim to be the supporters of real freedom. Further, many of us have assumed that freedom means "live and let live," but recently we decided that it did not mean let Naziism live. For a while, freedom meant just about everything and anything and therefore nothing in particular. Now, under pressure and violent disagreements, we are finding it necessary to define freedom more precisely.

Our problem is the same as that of the early Christian Church; that is, how to define our values and beliefs so that they will not be too empty and vague on the one hand, nor too narrow and dictatorial on the other hand. Thus, the Church had to make up its mind and say, in effect, here is the set of Doctrines of God, which seem to be consistent with each other, based on the New Testament and the experiences of Christians. This set is not in itself complete or exhaustive, but it is cohesive and integrated. In our opinion, other doctrines put forth do not reflect either our experiences nor meet with the logic of our doctrines and therefore we will have to say that they cannot fairly claim the label Christian. This is an unpleasant and difficult task, and the possibility of error must be admitted. But any other course would lead to disaster. For no organization in life can operate in any other way. No state can allow any members to do anything they want to do—in the name of freedom. We are not free to rob, murder, sabotage and destroy. We have values and laws, and these define our freedom and its limits.

So in religion, there must be some limits to a man's behavior and beliefs if he is to be a member "in good standing." To be sure, the Church has often erred in the direction of being too narrow, but it can also err in the direction of too much latitude and so become dissipated. It could become all things to all men, it could mean everything and therefore nothing at all. The problem is that very difficult tight-rope between tyranny of dogma on the one hand, and meaningless generalizations on the other hand. Some well-meaning but naive people have overlooked this problem when they loudly proclaim the need and facility of a one-world religion. There is an apocryphal story told about such a person who set out to find the common denominator upon which all the world's religions could agree. He spent thirty years studying the various religions and finally discovered two principles which everybody could agree on, and so there was the real possibility of just one universal religion. The two principles of universal agreement were: (1) Religion may be defined as "an awareness of God"—if there is one; (2) Life is worth living—sometimes!

There *is* diversity in religion as in all other areas of life. Some of the differences are needless and tragic. But some are inevitable and healthy. No view of God is complete, but not all views of God are equally true. The problem is to have a meaningful and true set of beliefs about God, but also to keep such a set dynamic; that is, subject to constant re-examination, re-interpretation, and re-application. A flat, literal acquiescence, or uncritical worship of dogmas leads to stagnation and persecution. Ignorance and reckless rejection of historic dogma lead to meaningless generalizations and dissipation of vigor and guidance. Christians want neither a unity of meaningless principles nor the unity of a dictator. Protestant theologians seek to retain the difficult and endless search for diversity within unity, and know that this search never reaches a static level where they can then say, "We've got it." There will and must always be diversity, especially in knowledge of God and in statements about God. This is why I believe theology at its best is dynamic rather than static. This is why I believe in the limitations of theology as well as in its growth.

On the other hand, to those who feel that there is an absolute difference between all religions, I would suggest this: that while there are differences and viewpoints which are obviously contradictory, nevertheless there are some basic unities of fundamental importance. Even from a strictly sociological approach to the world's great religions, it must be admitted that vast numbers of people have had certain experiences which they believed to be directly involved with some aspect of ultimate reality. Regardless of how we moderns look at these experiences, these people had religious experiences in which *they* (rightly or wrongly from our point of view) believed was an experience of a power greater than and beyond them, but which was operating in and through them. Further, these people believed this power to be the ultimate power or powers of the Universe. All the world's great religions began with this type of religious experience. This is why religion is defined by authorities in most fields as "an awareness of or belief in power or powers greater than the individual" or belief in "the determiner of one's destiny."

In short, all religion is born out of some discovery of power beyond man yet operating in and through man. This is an empirical fact which is of immense significance and one that is overlooked by many students of sociology, anthropology and religion. There is a common religious experience that seems to be well-nigh universal in mankind. The commonality, therefore, among all religions is not doctrinal but experiential. Differences appear between the religions in their descriptions and definitions of these experiences. The power that is felt may be defined as the rain god—Kismet, Atman, Jehovah, God. In explaining the power and in trying to share and communicate it to others, the power is sometimes made too concrete. Hence, this power may be defined as residing in a purple cow, or totem pole, or chalice, or on Mt. Olympus. These are obvious differences, but what is common is the experience which is so real to the believers. All the rest of the story of how each religion was organized, manipulated by priests, corrupted by economic, political and sociological forces, is all perfectly true. But this later historical development should not hide the original fact of *what* caused religions to appear in the first place. Man's religious experience of God, however defined, seems to be inevitable. The religious history of mankind, therefore, is, in essence, the history of man's experience of the ultimate power or reality in life and his description of it. And as in all other fields of history, one can easily trace the growth from primitive origins to more modern and mature developments. But the thread is discernible throughout—a common experience. It is this fact, too often neglected by both religious and secular folk alike, which should prevent us from self-righteous controversy with those who have different definitions of God.

The Christian view of God, like other religious views of God, is partly derived from the long and varied religious experiences of men. In addition, it is based on the primary conviction—also partly derived from experience—that God revealed Himself most fully in Jesus Christ. Nevertheless, Christian theology is a system of beliefs about God. At the same time, while I believe it is the most adequate definition and description of God that is available, I do not believe it to be complete. Therefore, Christian theology, if true to itself, welcomes other views, and criticizes what it already has. Theology, like all of the Christian life, is a search and a pilgrimage. But like all journeys, the pilgrim has some knowledge of where he is going, what he is looking for, and what it means to engage in the adventure. That is why Christians speak of God as "the author and finisher of our faith."

7

DOCTRINE OF CHRIST

IN THE previous chapter on the Doctrine of God, several statements were made without explaining how Christianity could arrive at such conclusions. For example, it was said that the Christian faith holds that God is Love, and that God revealed Himself most fully in the person of Jesus of Nazareth. Such statements cannot be explained or substantiated without a full discussion of the nature of Christ. Indeed, this problem, who or what was Jesus Christ (called "the Christological Problem"), is perhaps *the* central problem in the Christian religion. One might even go so far as to say that almost all other doctrines and problems in Christianity are derived from the Christological problem. Thus, it seems fair to say that the primary question throughout Christian history has been "Who was Jesus Christ and what difference does He make?" One's belief in Christianity largely depends on the answer; one's theological position stems directly from whatever answer is given.

Historically, it is safe to say that Christianity begins with Christ. This is not to say that Christianity has no roots or background in Judaism and other religious traditions. It is only to say that Jesus was the figure who was responsible for the birth of the Christian religion and that His disciples and apostles organized the faith in response to the nature of Christ. They had to decide this problem of Christ. Since the time of the apostles many different answers have been given.

114

But in spite of the varying views, the Church was founded on and has maintained throughout history one agreed-upon view; namely, that God was in Christ. Today there are other interpretations given.

One of these views states that Jesus was the Great Teacher or Prophet. This view is held by Judaism but also by many other people, some Protestants, some humanists, some of no particular religious affiliation. This interpretation sees Jesus as entirely human with no divine qualities, other than those any other man might have. His contribution was great, as many other great teachers and prophets before and after contributed much. Jesus as a teacher gave us some interesting moral and spiritual insights and ideas. He obviously contributed to the moral advance of mankind by influencing Western culture. He is to be revered along with other great men, like Isaiah, Jeremiah, Aristotle, Plato, and Buddha. This view, moreover, would also insist that Jesus, shorn of later Church dogmas about Him, would still remain a man, subject to all the limitations of any man, great or small. Thus, Jesus did not know all things; He made mistakes in judgment, prophesied incorrectly. He was angry, He suffered, He did not want to die, and not all of His teachings were practical or wise. And certainly, those who held this view would say the Resurrection story is a later creation by the excited followers of Christ, improved upon by formulators of Church dogma. This view is not put forth in any derogatory fashion by its proponents. They are merely attempting to strip away what seems to be later interpretations, and to establish the full humanity of Jesus. And humanity is not established by picturing a great man as being totally without limitations, problems, and mistakes that all other human beings have. Therefore, Jesus is indeed the Great Teacher, a great man among other great men, but still a man. If this is true, then it is quite consistent not to worship Jesus as a

God, nor to elevate Him too highly over other noble figures in history. This interpretation of Jesus is quite correct in not idolizing Christ, nor regarding Him as the Saviour. For no one man can save the world, nor save even one person. Thus, this view prefers to collect the wisdom from *all* the great teachers and sages without pretending that one had some unique stature or nature that was unlike all other human beings.

A second view of Jesus, which is similar, may be called the Relativistic view. This position holds also that there was nothing special nor divinely unique about Jesus. He was simply another good man in history. He had some good ideas, some not so good. He was subject to most of the temptations that other human beings experience. He was a "good" man because He had "good" ideas, tried to practice them, and had the courage of His convictions to die for them. But other men in history have done this, too—Socrates and thousands of martyrs in all ages. Therefore, Jesus is to be respected, His contributions to be considered. But there are no grounds for elevating Him to the status of being Divine, or a God, or of uncritical worship of Him. This view is largely shared by people outside of Christianity. It might be termed the modern secular view.

A third view may be labelled the Humanist-Perfectionist approach. This interpretation sees Jesus as the Perfect Man, the best man that ever lived. Jesus was the Ideal Man, the one man in history who is the model for all other men, the one person whom all should strive to imitate. Equally important as the man Jesus are His teachings which were simple yet noble. With intelligence and education, mankind can approach, and one day fulfill, the wisdom of Jesus. Further, His ideas, perfectly exemplified by Jesus' own life, are not the property of any one religion or denomination, but are so broad and simple that all men can live by them without all the paraphernalia of ritual and institutionalism. Yet this view, like the previous two, would also insist that there was nothing magical or divine about Jesus. Though He was not perfect, He was entirely human. He differs from the rest of us in the degree of His perfection, but there is no qualitative or radical difference between us. This view is held largely by "liberal Protestants," such as, in general, Congregationalists, Unitarians, and many other individuals among the other denominations. It is also held by humanists of various kinds, and by exponents of other secular views such as idealism.

These labels, "humanism," "secular," are highly debatable and must be used with reservation and qualification. As used here, "humanism" means, generally, the belief that mankind, however constituted, can work out its own salvation. Such a belief does not necessarily exclude God, who is usually defined as a given partner of man in the enterprise of life. "Secular" is used here to denote the view which holds that mankind can work out its destiny without a God, or the view that God is to be defined largely in terms of natural process. Both humanists and secularists, as here described, see no necessity for the Church in its historic institutional form, nor do they find much sympathy with the "orthodox" theological doctrines. These unreliable labels are not meant to be used in any disparaging fashion. It should be obvious that many devotees of these viewpoints are filled with high ideals, firm convictions, fidelity of purpose and live out their beliefs with great intensity; so much so, in many instances, as to shame orthodox Christians. My purpose here is only to use labels to distinguish different interpretations of the nature of Christ.

The three views described all too briefly above, are among the most widely shared interpretations of Jesus today. Like all such opinions, they can be supported by an immense amount of scholarly fact, detailed research, and historical evidence. They are not mere fancies, superficial opinions, nor institutional dogma. Having said this, it must also be noted that, in the last analysis, each view rests on faith, on some initial criterion or presupposition. Each view is a compound of fact and faith. Why and how this is so will be elaborated now in the historic "orthodox" view of Jesus Christ.

The orthodox or classical view of Jesus Christ, as stated in the Creeds and theology of the Church, both Roman Catholic and Protestant, ancient and modern, is that Jesus was both fully man and fully divine; He was the God-Man. The description of Jesus as the God-Man is the central idea or concept of this interpretation. In order to explain the meaning of this concept, various other terms were used by the Church in the past: "Son of God," "one substance with the Father," "Saviour," "The Christ," "Lord." These terms, appearing in different contexts in religious history, were vehicles for expressing the central view of Jesus as the God-Man. And while the arguments were often long, detailed and bitter, all Christians in the main stream of Christian thought used these words to describe their position on the Christological problem. The formal term for the concept of Jesus as the God-Man is the Doctrine of the Incarnation. The Doctrine of Christ and the Doctrine of the Incarnation are virtually the same in orthodox Christian theology. The meaning of these doctrines requires considerable explanation.

First of all, it must be admitted that to the modern mind especially, any such statement that Jesus of Nazareth was both fully God and fully man, that He was God incarnate and therefore essentially different from all other men, seems ludicrous, if not insulting to our intelligence. This is by way of saying that Christianity admits that this doctrine is a very difficult one, that it taxes our logic and, indeed, goes beyond empirical data and rational proof. As will be indicated, however, the doctrine is based, in part, on empirical data and rational order, but it is also a matter of faith. Granting, then, that this is a very difficult doctrine to understand, what can be said for it in order to clarify the meaning? Let us begin with the historical and empirical evidence.

The Gospel records, thoroughly examined by scholars of all convictions, give us the story of Jesus of Nazareth—little about His early life, but a fair amount concerning His later life and teachings, and much about the reactions and experiences of those who knew Jesus or were influenced by Him. Non-Christian sources give brief mention to a Jesus "who is called the Christ." Seventy-five years ago there were some who held that there never was a Jesus of Nazareth, but this view has been thoroughly refuted by historians and scholars in and outside of Christianity. The amount of scientific research and historical analysis in the field of New Testament literature, the life of Jesus, and the social conditions of the time, is staggering. It is fair to say that probably no other figure nor period in history has received such a thorough and critical analysis. As a result, there is indisputable testimony and universal agreement on the fact that Jesus did live and acted in the manner reported by the Gospel records. Again, this says nothing about whether Jesus was God incarnate or not. All it says is there was a person from Nazareth who did certain things, said certain things, and had a certain influence on people. The problem of who Jesus was, or what His nature was or what is the full meaning of some of His actions and ideas—these questions constitute another set of problems. That He was born, lived, spoke, influenced, and died, are beyond dispute. That is why the three interpretations of Christ, described above, are at least partly true. There is no doubt that Jesus was a teacher, a better-than-average teacher in His time. There is no doubt that He was also a kind of prophet, more influential than the run-of-the-mill professional prophets of that time. There is no doubt that He was an unusual man worthy of the label "great." He was a great man, like other great men, in that He had some noble ideas, lived them out in His life, and indeed died for His convictions. Mankind has recognized Him as worthy and great. This much about Jesus is certainly historically true and recognized by people of all religions or no religions. And Christianity, of course, goes along with this, too.

Next, there is abundant evidence that the effect of Jesus on His disciples and followers was unusual. The large groups of people who saw and heard Jesus probably did not regard Him as anything but another minority leader of some stature, but little more. They were used to "friends of the people," religious prophets of encouragement, or political radicals offering hope of release from Roman occupation. Jesus was acclaimed as one of these, but certainly not regarded as divine.

The record suggests that there were other people, individuals and small groups who regarded Jesus as endowed with unusual spiritual gifts of healing and insight. These people, if they were familiar with their own heritage of Judaism (and most of them were), began to rank Jesus as another prophet, possibly another "special agent" from God. And among a minority of this smaller group of people, there doubtless was some talk of whether Jesus was the long-hoped-for Messiah—the saviour of Israel.

Finally, there were a few individuals and the disciples of Jesus who experienced extraordinary responses in their frequent and daily contacts with Jesus. It is only natural to expect that those intimately associated with Jesus would know Him better and have a variety of experiences. The Gospel record tells us of certain individuals, like Nicodemus, who were convinced rather rapidly that Jesus was perhaps divine. The story of Nicodemus, and ones similar to it, however, are not too reliable and the sketchy evidence is convincing neither way. The most one can say for them in terms of witnessing to the unusual character of Jesus, is, "Possibly!" While they are not too reliable, viewed as individual stories, when taken as part of the whole Gospel testimony, they merely add "possible credence," but certainly not clear proof.

Of course, the largest and most important evidence is the disciples themselves. It is clear that, in the beginning, the followers of Jesus saw Him as a great teacher, another prophet, a great man. They were attracted by His personality, His religious spirit and dedication, the authority of His convictions. But as they worked with Him, they began to sense that perhaps Jesus was more than just another great religious man. Just what more He was, they could not determine immediately. Finally, it was Peter who blurted out, "Thou art the Christ." In saying this, Peter was perhaps expressing his feeling that Jesus was the long-sought Messiah sent by God to redeem the world through Israel. If the record is accurate, Jesus replied that He was, but that Peter was not to tell anybody else. The reason for secrecy on this point is reasonably clear. There were many current views of the Messiah among the Jews.

One of the most popular at this time was the political view. According to this interpretation, the Messiah would be a political leader who would organize the Jews and overthrow the Roman domination and then lead his people to new triumphs of independent freedom and prosperity. This was decidedly not Jesus' view of the Messiah nor of His own role. The evidence suggests that Jesus' view of the Messiah was that of the Suffering Servant, as described in the Book of Isaiah (Chap. 53). But the problem of the nature of the Messiah is not discussed at all in the Gospels. The disciples seemed to regard Jesus as something most extraordinary, somehow divinely unique. Their daily experiences with Jesus convinced them that they were in the presence of God, that because of Jesus, they knew and felt God's power more completely and really.

It is most significant that Jesus did not use the so-called miracles to convince them. He did not try to amaze them or overrule any objections by waving a magic wand. He did not try to enforce His ideas by working wonders and signs. Whatever unusual events Jesus performed, He did them quietly, often away from the crowd, and always as examples of faith. He did not cure anyone against his will; He did not say, "Watch this one—this will really prove I'm something special." In each instance He used His powers to demonstrate the power of faith in God. He always raised the question of faith first, then proceeded to the cure, and ended with the admonition not to spread the news of the cure to the populace, for Jesus knew miracles would be misinterpreted and that the public soon would clamor for all kinds of signs. He would be acclaimed a necromancer, a wonder-worker, and people would thereby miss the whole point of His message and life. The disciples, of course, saw these miracles, but they were also taught their real significance; they were simply and solely a demonstration of the power of faith in God.

These miracles do not tell us much about the nature and character of Christ. It is for this reason that later Christian theology, at its best, has never used "the miracles of Jesus" as proof of His divinity. In so doing, theology has been faithful to the New Testament. For the New Testament interprets the miracles as partial evidences, or examples, of the power of God, not as "proofs" about the nature of Christ. Today, the wisdom of this interpretation can be reasonably verified. We now know enough about "faith healing" to know that any trained person can effect this type of healing, that certain ailments which we now label "psychosomatic" can be greatly helped by therapy which aids a person in achieving inner attitudes of trust (faith), peace of mind and serenity. Incidentally, the New Testament records that the disciples, and later the apostles, engaged in many faith-healing cures. Therefore, it is clear that this ability was not unique with Christ. As will be noted later, whether Jesus was in some sense divine or not, does not rest on the miracles.

To return attention to the disciples of Jesus, it may be said that they were undoubtedly impressed with the miracles, but that the relationship between them and Jesus was not dependent upon the miracles. What assured the devotion and fidelity of the disciples to Jesus was not so much what He *did*, but what He *was*. As in any other human relationship, understanding and affection is not generated by one or two unusual deeds; it is cultivated by the *total* personality and its total impact on other people. Thus, to the disciples, Jesus' total personality impressed them in an extraordinary fashion. To them, He seemed to be divine. Somehow, some way, they could not explain or define, Jesus seemed to be more than a man. Or, to put it another way, through Jesus, because of Jesus, God seemed to be present more vividly, more really than in any other way they had ever known.

But, as the Gospels record the stories, this awareness and belief came to an abrupt end—temporarily. With the trial and crucifixion of Jesus, it was quite normal for the disciples to decide that they were mistaken. For if Jesus was somehow God incarnate, His untimely death could not substantiate their impression. It was axiomatic that God could not die. If Jesus was in some manner God incarnate, this tragedy could not have happened. But it did. Therefore, they concluded that Jesus was not God. Accordingly, the disciples fled in all directions, bitter, disillusioned, and intensely aware of what seemed to be their erroneous impression of the nature of Christ. Then the New Testament describes the amazing account of the Resurrection. We shall take up this fascinating and difficult problem in the next chapter. But at this point, regardless of what we believe about the Resurrection, the evidence about the behavior of the disciples is clear. Scattered and disillusioned, they believed that Jesus in some fashion arose from the dead and appeared in their midst, to them personally, and therefore Jesus was not dead but raised up, alive. This dramatic and overpowering experience, identical in all the disciples (save Judas) brought them together again, reconfirmed their view of Jesus as the Christ, and made them spend the rest of their lives in complete and utter devotion to spreading the "good news of Christ"—even unto death.

As will be discussed later, it is difficult to explain this recovery from bitterness and the long period of missionary fervor that followed merely as an hallucination. There may have been elements of hallucination in some of the experiences, but hallucinations do not last, nor do they produce the steady and constant personality structure that remained throughout the lives of the disciples. At any rate, the historical evidence still remains that "something" happened which produced men who organized and spread a new religion.

These men believed that God was in Christ and that therefore what Christ revealed to them was true. That is why the central message of the disciples and apostles was not the Sermon on the Mount, but the proclamation, derived from their own vivid experiences, that Jesus, who was crucified, is not dead but alive. Therefore, God reigns, God acts, He has revealed Himself by this deed to man. This was the good news—that God has cared enough for mankind to reveal Himself to men through Jesus of Nazareth. Now, therefore, we know more about God, more about His nature and purpose, His will for us. For we have "seen Him in the flesh." This is the supreme good news.

Such was the claim and the teaching of the early church. But how do we know this is true? How did they know it was true? This is the crucial problem for moderns. It is essentially the problem of evidence and the problem of knowing. The only evidence we have on this whole problem is the written evidence of the Gospels and the letters of Paul. The other written evidence in the New Testament and early Christian theology is statements about the problem, interpretations, and derived meanings. But it is only in Matthew, Mark, Luke, Acts, and John, that we have accounts of Jesus' life and teachings and the reactions of the disciples. As noted previously, this literature has been raked over with a fine, critical comb, so that today we know quite well the authenticity of each document. Scholars have established with reasonable accuracy when each book was written, when later edited, what was omitted, what is common to all the documents, what Jesus probably said, and what he very likely did not say. Research has enabled us to separate what was perhaps historical fact from what was probably a useful fable or interpretation of some event, though this endeavor is indeed limited.

But our central problems remain. We do not have any written records put down in Jesus' own handwriting. We do not have any information from an "objective historian" of the period. All our records were written by men with a "point of view," by convinced Christians. Most of the documents were written with a special purpose to some particular audience. But we know what the "slant" was and who was the audience. We know also that each author used the same sources and material, but drew upon additional information and presented a case. Therefore, there is no clear-cut "objective view" of Christ. There is no "facts about Christ" on the one hand, and somebody's subjective interpretation of these facts on the other hand. Fact, near-fact, and interpretation are all mixed together. This is why there can never be a purely unbiased historical account of Jesus. There is no document on which it could be based.

Some moderns still believe that it is possible to "get behind" all the interpretations and records and arrive at a clear, objective, and factual picture of the "simple Jesus." This has been labelled, "The Helicopter View of Jesus" (Paul Lehmann). But there is no way to get behind the present evidence. When it comes to the problem of how one decides whether God was in Christ, whether this was the Incarnation, the only evidence we have are the assertions of the disciples, apostles and Gospel writers. And they seem to agree that God was, in some way, in Christ, that a Resurrection of some kind did occur, that therefore God did act in history.

Our point, therefore, is that the evidence for the belief in the Incarnation is overwhelmingly in behalf of it. The New Testament documents all attest in one way or another to the interpretation that God was in Christ. At the same time, this does not "prove" the interpretation. We are thus in the position of having a set of evidences which is a compound of fact, experience and faith. We have no set of evidences to the contrary. From a strictly scientific point of view, therefore, the issue of the nature of Christ *cannot be settled either way*. There is no objective, historical evidence that Jesus was only a man or was the incarnate of God. Yet attempts have been made to settle the problem in both directions by the historical method. Such endeavors have not stood rigorous examination.

Some critics have tried to prove that Jesus was simply a

man. In so doing, they have taken the New Testament evidence and stripped it of all interpretation. The claim is made, therefore, that nothing but the bare "facts" remain. Other critics have pointed out, however, that it is not possible to separate "bare facts" from interpretations, personal experiences, and convictions. How can one decide that another person's experience is a "fact" or an illusion, or a mixture of both? As soon as one makes judgments about the content of a man's experience, he is operating from some point of view. Thus, when the Gospels record the experiences of the disciples—their impressions of, or reactions to, Christ—the authors are assuming the validity of these experiences. The events and content are real to the disciple and because the Gospel writers hold the same point of view, they also assume validity in the experiences of the disciples. But, when someone else challenges the New Testament interpretation, he is making the challenge from another point of view. The key point is that the data available is the same. What one does with the New Testament data depends upon one's beliefs or presuppositions. One cannot prove the nature of Christ by some new fact or evidence outside the New Testament. There is no new twentieth century fact or set of evidences which enable us to prove one way or another what the nature of Jesus was.

This controversy has been going on a long time. Our chief purpose here is to point out that the problem cannot be settled scientifically. The religionist is wrong if he claims scientific, historical proof for the Divinity of Jesus; the secularist is wrong if he claims similar proof for the mere humanity of Jesus. The only fair position for a strict secularist to take is the statement that Jesus was a man and that whether He was something more than a man cannot be determined one way or another by the scientific method. The only fair statement for the religionist is to say that scientific investigation proves the existence and humanity of Jesus, but that belief in Christ as something more than a man is determined only partly by evidences and partly by one's faith. For us moderns, this point needs to be stressed, for our temptation is to think that anyone who sees Jesus as another great man and in no sense divine, is viewing Jesus from an unbiased position. Such is not the case. For this is a judgment based on the faith either that there is no God or that God could not act in this way. Such faith cannot be proved or disproved scientifically, either. It is a faith. The real argument, therefore, between those who believe God was in Christ and those who believe Jesus to be only a man is an argument between two different faiths. It is *not* an argument between "science and religion."

Let us now see why and how a Christian can arrive at the view that God was in Christ, that Jesus was the God-Man. We have already stressed how the disciples and apostles felt that in knowing Jesus they came to know God more clearly, that when they were in the presence of Jesus they felt they were in the presence of God, and that after the Resurrection these experiences seemed to be confirmed. The New Testament literature is a recording of these experiences as well as a record of part of Jesus' life and teachings. The writings describe how and why these first Christians arrived at their convictions about the nature of Jesus and God. For the whole message of Jesus was the proclamation of God—His nature, His power, His purpose for Man. The center of attraction was not simply Jesus as man but the God revealed through and by Jesus. And, indeed, the disciples experienced precisely that God. We cannot deny them these experiences. But the problem for all Christians after the disciples and first apostles is, how do *we* know that Jesus was the

Christ? This was the problem of the early Christians who had not seen Jesus; it was the problem of the third-century Christians; it is the problem of the twentieth-century Christians. How do we know who Christ was?

The historic answer can be described briefly. From the first beginnings of the early Church the pattern is remarkably similar. The disciples and apostles, having experienced what they believed was the living God in Christ, shared their experiences with others. They went about telling and explaining the "good news of the Kingdom of God." Soon, the New Testament literature began to appear. The story was now being told both by word of mouth and by letters. Many people thus knew about it and came to believe it. Why? The most one can say is that the story made sense to them; it filled a need in their lives; it gave them meaning and power. How else can one explain why a person believes what he does? To be sure, these are general explanations and they do not tell us why these people believed Christianity rather than some other religion. To say that Christianity met a need is fair, but it doesn't explain why something else couldn't have filled the personal need just as well. It is probably impossible to determine accurately why a person adopts a new, mature religion.

At any rate, when acquainted with the Christian story, many people began to live according to the Christian faith and so came to experience God. Their testimony about the nature of God, how Christ was for them the avenue to God, is amazingly identical. A Christian in Italy speaks of "falling in love with Christ." At the same time, another Christian on the other side of the Mediterranean in Antioch even uses the same phrase—"falling in love with Christ." People from various cultures, in different lands, learn of the Christian faith and live it, then they "compare notes" and find that they are experiencing the same God, the same "living Christ." This community of shared meanings and experiences lends credibility to the faith.

And this has been the history of the growth of Christianity. People in all the centuries have become acquainted in one way or another with the Christian faith. They have tried it; some discarded it, others held on to it, and grew into it. Those who came to believe it have found that their experiences and interpretations of these events or feelings have been the same as those of other Christians now and throughout Church history. It is very real to them, and since so many others have testified the same way, they feel that it must be true. I know of no other way in which one could test the validity of any faith. Any person in love knows how hard it is to describe the nature of love and what it does for him, what it means to him. Yet he would steadfastly deny that his love is unreal and mere illusion. He cannot prove in any scientific sense his love and his meaning. All he can do is to say again and again, using various symbols, what he means. Still, to an outsider, he may make no headway. And, indeed, an impasse is often reached.

Suppose, for example, we adopt the role of an agnostic. As agnostics, we may well reach this same impasse in our quest for understanding love. We will say that we simply do not know what the man in love means or what love is like. We may judge that he likes it; it seems to do him good, and all that, but for us, we do not really know what love is and why the man feels that way. We can ask him all kinds of questions about proving his love, demonstrating that it is more than an Oedipus situation. The fact is that he cannot prove all this in scientific terms. What shall we conclude? If we say that there is no such thing as love, we have made an unscientific leap and come up with a dogma. If we are true to our agnostic position we can come to no conclusion. We would say, simply, that love seems to be powerful and meaningful to a person in love, but it means nothing to us, and we still do not know very much about it. So our impasse is reached. The only way this block can be overcome is to fall in love ourselves. The only real answer, or rather, plea that a person in love may make, is to say, "When you are in love, then and only then will you know what I mean."

What I am saying, then, is that one has to have experiences of love in order to know what it is all about. Human love is like that. One has to love and be loved to know about it. Religion is like that. One has to be inside of a faith to grasp its power and meaning, or lack of it.

On the problem of Christ, the issue is the same. We cannot prove scientifically the nature of Christ; we cannot demonstrate it by logical argument. All we can point to is the Gospel account which records the fact that the disciples and apostles who knew Christ felt that He was more than a man. The meanings they gave agreed that He was in some sense "Divine." And this evidence has since been corroborated by the experience and interpretation of thousands of Christians. What is common to all these people is that in coming to know Jesus they have come to know God more fully. In their experience of Christ, they experienced God. This is the New Testament record; this is the witness of the Church ever since. This cannot be proved scientifically to the outsider. This is why the invitation to the Christian religion has always been faith first, which means at this point: Since faith in the God we know in Christ has been so meaningful for so many, come, join us and see if it is not also meaningful to you. One learns about love only if he launches out on the faith that there is such a thing as love and that it is worth seeking. In religion, one launches out only on the faith that there is a God and that He can be known and that such knowledge is worth-while. In both instances, there is evidence that other people have found it helpful. But whether I personally will find it so is my own venture of faith.

Is Christ the God-Man? The answer is partly the experiences of others and partly faith. In the last analysis, it can only be answered from inside of the Christian faith. The problem cannot be settled from outside, any more than human love can be settled from the outside. So the real answer to the question is this: If we are not in Christianity, the honest answer would seem to be the agnostic one of, "I don't know," with weight on the very doubtful side. If we are inside of the Christian faith, the answer throughout Christian history is that Christ is the God-Man. Yet a basic problem still remains. We have not said why this doctrine is still important and central today. Let us then try and see why this is important and what Christianity means when it speaks of Christ as the God-Man.

The label God-Man is the Church's attempt to explain its belief that God invaded history in the person of Jesus of Nazareth, that thereby God revealed Himself most clearly to men. The New Testament tries to say this in many ways. From the point of view of the New Testament, the Old Testament is regarded as the record of religious prophets who had expected some kind of special revelation of God. The prophets felt that God revealed His righteous law to Moses and that His moral purposes could be deduced from historical events. They also believed, along with the Psalmists, that God's handiwork could be seen in the order and design of nature. But in addition, the prophets seemed to feel that somehow, some way, God would reveal much more of Himself. They were not sure just how. Some thought He would send a special agent, a Messiah, Son of God; others thought some man, like David, might be given special powers, but the more profound prophets felt that God Himself would appear perhaps in the form of a man, perhaps not as a triumphant kind but as a suffering servant. Indeed, the Old Testament story is marked by a sense of great expectation of some special revelation of God.

The New Testament writers, fully aware of the prophets, tried to indicate that Jesus was the fulfillment of this expectation. The experiences of the disciples seemed to confirm this. Hence, many of the Old Testament terms are used in the New Testament. Jesus is called the Messiah, Son of God, Son of Man, and Lord. In trying to convey the same idea to Greek people in the philosophy of the Greeks, the Gospel of John describes Jesus as "the Word (Truth) made flesh." These labels have been the subject of great controversy amongst the scholars, and detailed analysis has tried to determine whether the Hebrew use of the word "Messiah" had any divine connotations or not.

The controversies still go on. In this writer's opinion, the issue cannot be settled by historical analysis, for, as may be suspected, the scholars agree on the evidences but disagree on the interpretations. Thus, one has scholars on both sides, but the position of each side is determined not by the evidences, but by private convictions. It seems clear to this writer that the New Testament authors were unanimous in their conviction that Jesus was in some way the incarnation of God and that each writer tried to convey this by using symbols familiar to his audience, symbols which conveyed some idea of divinity. I have no doubt that they would differ in detail as to just how or in what special way Jesus was God on earth. Indeed, there will doubtless always be and ought to be differences on this point. But it does seem clear that the New Testament writers were agreed that Jesus was in some way the fulfillment of the Old Testament expectation, and that He was in some way God revealing Himself in a special way. And this affirmation has been central to orthodoxy since the New Testament period. The creeds and theology of the Church similarly have confirmed this conviction. As time went on, other labels were used, new controversies arose, and then newer labels had to be invented. The problem is still with us. Yet the central Christian affirmation remains the same: that God revealed Himself to man in the person of Jesus. What varies and will continue to vary is the explanation of how this is possible.

Today, the chief argument seems to be why this central Doctrine of the God-Man is necessary at all. Most moderns do not believe it and regard it as unnecessary, if not "old-fashioned," and outmoded.

Why, then, does Christian theology retain this doctrine? The primary reason concerns the problem of how we know God. This, of course, is an age-old question in all religions. To the query, "How do I find God?" the Church has always replied, in effect, "If you want to know God most clearly, look at Jesus Christ. For in Christ, God revealed Himself most clearly." This is the keystone of the Christian faith. If this doctrine is not maintained, consider some of the alternatives.

In the first place, if God did not reveal Himself in Jesus, what do we know about God? The answer is that we know only what other religions prior to Jesus offer us. This means that the Christian religion offers nothing new to our knowledge of God.

In the second place, if Jesus was only a man, from what criterion do we judge Him to be a great teacher? If we say He gave us new insights into the nature of God, by what standard do we determine these ideas to be new? His ideas may be different, but are they true? In order to say that His views are true, we must know already what is truth. I doubt if this is a tenable position for any honest man.

In the third place, the underlying issue is the question of

authority. If Jesus was only a human being, by what authority can He speak of the nature of God? The answer is that He would have no special right that is not available to any other man. Similarly, the question must also be put to us. By what authority do we judge Jesus' ideas of God to be true? The answer to this question brings us back to the problem of revelation. In the chapter on Revelation it was stated that God cannot be proved by reference to some other criterion. Revelation, like light, is self-authenticating. Man either accepts it, or he does not. God was in Christ, or He was not. If God was present in Jesus, there is authority for accepting Jesus and His teachings as a way of life. If God was not present in Jesus, there is no authority for following Jesus. The importance today of the Christian Doctrine of Jesus Christ as the God-Man, then, is to meet the perennial questions of how one knows God and by what authority Christians try to follow Jesus.[1]

In summary, it is the Christian faith, derived from the experiences of the disciples and apostles that God was in Christ, that through Christ, man can come to know God more fully and completely, that thereby God revealed Himself, incarnated Himself in the person of Jesus of Nazareth. That is why Jesus is called the God-Man, or Savior, or Redeemer. This is where Christianity begins. This is *the central* conviction of the Christian faith.

[1] For an examination of the various contemporary theological views on the Doctrine of Christ, see Appendix A.

8

DOCTRINE OF THE RESURRECTION

I F THE Christian Doctrine of Christ is difficult, the
Christian Doctrine of the Cross and the Resurrection
is much more so. Many sensitive moderns can understand why Christians believe they see God more
clearly in Jesus of Nazareth than in any other figure in history. Indeed, many of us might well agree that whatever we
know about God we know through people, and perhaps most
supremely through Jesus. In the previous chapter, we described humanists who agree to this idea; namely, that if
there is a God, He must certainly be known primarily
through a person or persons. However, when we come to the
idea of the Resurrection, most moderns part company with
Christians.

At first glance, the evidence seems to be all on the side of
modernity. In our age of science, with all its advances and
knowledge, especially in biology, it would seem ridiculous
for any honest person to believe that Jesus was crucified,
dead, and buried, and then rose again on the third day. All
the biological evidence seems to be against such an event.
Every organism, human and animal, dies sometime. When it
dies, it is the end. Nobody comes to life again. There is no
evidence of any kind for such a phenomenon. Therefore, the
Christian story about a bodily Resurrection of Jesus is both
impossible and false. *This* doctrine is too much! We cannot
believe it! And yet Paul anticipated our attitude when he

said that the Resurrection was "foolishness to the Greeks and a stumbling block to the Jews." Are we to conclude, then, that Christianity is foolishness, that only fools believe it? Again, let us examine what evidences and arguments there are and see if we can at least try to understand the Christian idea of the Cross and the Resurrection, and why, even today, this doctrine remains so central.

A. *The Cross*

First, what are the historical facts? It is quite clear that Jesus of Nazareth was crucified, killed by being nailed to a cross. He was then removed from the cross, and His body was interred in some kind of a small cave. Presumably, large rocks were rolled up sealing off the entrance and guards set to watch. Some of the details will undoubtedly remain obscure. We shall probably never know definitely who buried Jesus. It might have been Joseph of Arimathea, or a group of friends. The burial was perhaps supervised by either the Romans or agents of the Sanhedrin. If a guard was set, it, too, was probably at the orders of Caiaphas. The crucifixion of Jesus was religious and political dynamite to the established Jewish hierarchy, and Caiaphas took no chances that anything "unusual" should happen. But this is only speculation. There are all kinds of questions we could ask about this situation. Did Joseph bury Jesus? If so, where? How do we know it was a large cave or a small cave? What was the name of the guard on the right side of the tomb? Did the Roman soldiers supervise the burial, etc.? The answer to all these and similar questions is: nobody knows for sure. The same kind of questions could be asked about any great historical figure—Socrates, Caesar, Napoleon—and no one can really answer such detailed queries. Yet there is still some factual evidence and some reasonable conclusions which can be drawn from the facts. Thus, all scholars agree on this much: that Jesus was killed by being crucified—a slow and agonizing form of torture. He died on the Cross, was taken down and buried in some tomb, which was sealed up, as was customary. What is important here is that Jesus was dead and buried.

Before proceeding further, the interpretation of these facts which Christian theology offers must be described. These views are often called "the theology of the Cross." One interpretation is this: the Cross is a symbol of part of life. The Cross thus stands as a reminder that good things are often crucified in life, that evil in many forms does appear triumphant over good, and that life has its tragic situations. The Cross, considered by itself and apart from the Resurrection, appears as a tragic symbol. In this context, Christianity sees the whole life of Jesus—His birth, youth, ministry and teachings, ending on Calvary. Moreover, if it is true that God was in some way working through Jesus, if it is true that what He said is the Truth, then what is the meaning of Jesus' early death? The meaning is that either we are totally wrong about Jesus and God, or else God and Christ were defeated and therefore impotent. Even if Jesus were only the "Good Man," or the "best that ever lived," the problem remains the same. Does not the death of this "great man" tend to suggest that evil wins out in life? Many other great men have been killed, many noble plans defeated, and great hopes for peace dashed into war.

Christianity sees the Cross as a realistic reminder of the power of evil in life. We further believe that a very good case can be made out for the idea that evil does win out in history. There is abundant evidence, ancient and modern. Or even in our own individual lives, a rigorous analysis might show us that most of our lives are but a series of disillusionments, changed plans, broken hopes, and frustrations. In Christian history, the stubborn fact is that Jesus the Christ was killed. And if this is the last chapter in the life of Christ, honesty requires us to conclude that life is essentially tragic and meaningless.

Yet it is also a fact that very few people in life ever come to this dismal conclusion. Why? There are many reasons, obviously, but the chief reason, I believe, is that we *do not want* to come to this conclusion. The vast majority of people *want* to find meaning and purpose in life. We do not want to believe that life is tragic and meaningless. Psychologically, we *must* believe that life makes sense—and so we do, regardless of the evidence. But *feeling* this way does not make it so. The realism of Christianity would insist that on the basis of personal and historical evidence, the pessimists have just as good a case as the optimists, and *within* Christian history up to the event of the Crucifixion, the pessimists have *all* the evidences. Integrity requires that we face up to the pessimist's challenge. And how can we honestly reply to such a charge? It will not do to say we "feel" that the pessimist is wrong, or that we just don't agree with him. Where is the evidence in history? Inside Christian history, where is the evidence? The answer in Christianity is: If the Cross is the last chapter, there isn't any reply. If Jesus died, then God lost and evil won.

For these reasons, Christianity at its best has always taken evil in life seriously and has always tried to meet squarely the problem of meaning in life in the face of evil. We shall see later (pp. 171 ff.) when we discuss the nature of evil, that this fundamental problem is the stumbling block for all philosophies and religions, including Christianity. This problem is the weakest link in all philosophical and theological systems. The way to pierce any proud intellect's armor is to ask about evil. This question will embarrass anyone. At least, Christianity takes the problem seriously even if it cannot produce a pat answer.

The Cross, then, throws down this basic challenge about the meaning of life: Does the good or evil win out? The answer, according to Christianity, is that the tragedy of Calvary suggests that life is basically evil. But, of course, the New Testament does not stop here. Something of a great consequence to all human beings happened after the Crucifixion.

B. *The Resurrection*

The Gospel record unanimously testifies that Jesus rose from the dead, appeared several times to the disciples, and later "rose up to Heaven." This is the nub of the Resurrection description; this is the fantastic story! What evidence have the scholars discovered to support this claim? It seems very clear that the reaction of the disciples to the Cross was one of complete disillusionment. With the death of their beloved Master, they fled in all directions. Most of them probably returned to Jerusalem; others left and set out for their respective villages. All seemed to be in a state of complete bewilderment. This tragedy could not have happened. They were convinced heart and soul that what Jesus preached was true: that God is the Lord of Life; that He is love; that His purposes were real and would triumph. Yet all this seemed to be vitiated by the Cross. It was all over. Truth was smashed. Little wonder, then, that the disciples were bewildered! For them, it was a time of despair and hopelessness.

Then, on the third day, the New Testament records how Jesus appeared again to the disciples. It is significant that the text recounts that Jesus appeared to each of them at different times, yet to none alone. That is to say, apparently Jesus was seen by two or three of the disciples together, and in the Upper Room in Jerusalem all together. What is significant about this is that their experiences of the risen Christ were the same. This fact tends to refute the idea that the disciples merely had hallucinations. It is difficult to maintain that eleven different men in different places at different times had exactly the *same* hallucination. It seems quite clear that some *objective* event occurred which alone accounts for the similarity of experiences. In addition, it is also clear that they compared "notes" so to speak, about their respective experiences and found that they agreed on the content of these events. "Did not our hearts burn within us" when we "saw Him?" they said, and the others nodded in agreement. This sharing of experience must have continued for some time. To be sure, we shall probably never know all the exact details, but a comparison of experiences is one of the best ways by which we may arrive at Truth. It is not the only test, nor is it complete in itself, but it is an indispensable part of validating anything in life.

Thus, regardless of one's views of the Resurrection, one is bound by integrity to consider the experiences of a group of men as well as the interpretations given to those experiences. What complicates our inquiry is that it is impossible to separate the *content* of the experience from the *interpretation* of the content. To say that the disciples were deluding themselves is a hasty and partial judgment—not a scientific statement. For how can one judge the *content* of a particular experience, especially when it occurred 2,000 years ago? On the other hand, one cannot assert *as a fact* that they experienced the risen Christ. This is an interpretation, a judgment, too. The only fact one can assert, is that *"something"* unusual did happen to the disciples; they did have an extraordinary experience. Precisely *what* the detailed nature of those experiences was, we shall never know as

scientific fact. At the same time, we have no reason to separate entirely interpretation from the content. This means
that we have to admit the possibility that *some* elements of
psychological illusion were present as well as other mental
processes. But it also means that we must entertain the possibility that something more than subjective ideas or feelings
was present. Not all psychological processes are unhealthy,
and reality can and does most often work *through* these
processes.

Furthermore, the distinction between a "vision" and "a
flash of insight" is often very obscure. The unconscious forces
may well have played a part in this situation, but who would
deny that God does not work through our unconscious life
as well as our conscious experience? Our point here is to
warn against too easy explanations. The experiences of the
disciples were real enough; they experienced "something."
Neither the agnostic nor the believer can definitely prove
by science that these experiences were nothing but illusion,
or nothing but the risen Christ. Our decision as to what we
believe about the disciples' experience depends ultimately
upon our own experiences of God and Christ and our faith,
that is, our interpretations. Thus, like the belief in Christ
as the Incarnation of God, it is a matter partly of fact, partly
of experience, and partly of interpretation and faith. It is
never one to the neglect of the others. And there are other
evidences and points to be considered.

It is significant that the New Testament describes the
appearances of Jesus as being different from His mortal
stature. When Jesus was seen by His disciples, His body
was different. The record only hints at it. But presumably
it was changed in some way and yet the Gospel accounts
emphatically deny that these appearances were pure spirit,
or ghost-like. Perhaps the doubting Thomas story happened,
perhaps not. But whether it did or not, it certainly reflects

the writer's desire to show that Jesus had some bodily characteristics, that He was no mere bit of divine ectoplasm, but a real person. This view of the risen Jesus as having real bodily substance coincides very closely with Paul's famous description of the Resurrection where, in I Corinthians 15, he speaks of a bodily resurrection, but one in which we shall be changed. Of course, Paul's Epistle was written earlier than any of the Gospels, yet he is describing what he believes will happen to all the faithful, while the Gospel writers are describing the interpretation given by the disciples of their experience of the risen Christ. It is doubtful that the writers borrowed the idea from Paul. It is more likely that the common experiences of the disciples and of Paul tended to verify each other. Everywhere in the New Testament it is clear that the description of the risen Christ suggests that His appearance was different than it had been during His earthly life. Yet He is seen neither as a ghost-like apparition nor as just another person. More than that we do not know. And this meager picture doubtless leaves us very sceptical. But more must be said in order to get a fuller understanding.

The New Testament is indeed vague in its literal description of what the resurrected Jesus looked like, but it continues with a rather full account of what happened to the disciples. It is certainly obvious that their experience of the risen Jesus was the most real and lasting experience of their whole lives. Regardless of all interpretations, the experiential facts can be summarized this way: After the death of Jesus, the disciples fled in despair and disillusionment. Then they experienced the risen and living Christ at least three times, compared their experiences, regained faith and meaning, banded together, founded the Church, and set out on a lifelong mission as ambassadors of the God they knew in Christ. Thus, it is clear that this experience of Jesus was not something that gave them a temporary "lift"; it had a permanent and lasting effect on their lives. So again, we are in the position of having some empirical data but no absolute proof. The credible evidence here is that it is unlikely that a mere set of illusions could have resulted in such a change in the disciples. The net effect of their experiences, in addition to the founding of the Church, was psychologically profound. Their lives were certainly integrated, purposive and powerful. They worked hard, grew in stature and maturity, and some endured martyrdom. There is no evidence that their resurrection experiences began a series of events which led to helpless neurosis. Quite the contrary, all the evidences point to a marked growth in maturity, vigor and creative living. This set of evidences seems to me to be the strongest support in favor of the validity of their resurrection experience.

There are other evidences to be considered. Of course, there is a difference between the resurrection appearances of Jesus shortly after His crucifixion and the later responses of Christians to "the living Christ." No claim is made by later Christians of having seen literally some bodily manifestation of Jesus. And the Gospel record does make this kind of claim. But it also states that after forty days, Jesus rose up into heaven, an event known as the Ascension. Presumably, therefore, the New Testament writers did not expect any more resurrection appearances, and their viewpoint seems to have been correct. No responsible Christian has ever made the claim of having seen the risen Christ in the same manner as did the disciples. Yet while there is this marked difference between the experiences of the disciples and those of later Christians, there is also an important similarity. Later Christians have had (and still do) the experience of "the living Christ." In a very real sense their "hearts burn within." The external object of Christ's body is not present, but the internal content seems to be the same as that of the disciples. In addition, the cause of the experience is not wholly subjective, for the antecedent factors were objective; namely, an acquaintance with the New Testament picture of Jesus, the observance of how other Christians act, and some prior experiences of God. Furthermore, the effects of this experience of the living Christ are almost always the same as those of the disciples. We described how the Resurrection experiences affected the disciples, how they were integrated, and renewed in strength and purpose. Similarly, later Christians were affected the same way. It is reasonable to conclude, therefore, that the content of the experiences was much the same, even though the detailed appearances varied. From the Christian point of view, then, there is abundant empirical data which is sufficiently similar both in causes and effects as to lend considerable validity to the assertion that Jesus Christ is not dead but alive.

Another interesting fact is that both the disciples and early apostles based most of their missionary work on the resurrection appearances. In contrast with much of today's preaching, the message of the early Christians was not the Golden Rule and the Ten Commandments; it was not even so much the teachings of Jesus as it was primarily the Doctrine of the Resurrection.

The chief sermon of these early churchmen was, "Jesus the Christ who was crucified, dead and buried, is not dead, but alive, raised up and reigneth forevermore." The more one reflects upon the announcement and its relation to the culture of the Roman world at that time, the more incredible the story becomes. Who, for example, could predict that such a story would appeal to the stoical Roman, or to the philosophically-minded Greek? Christianity did not attract merely the ignorant and the superstitious. This is what one would expect with the Resurrection story. The fact is that it attracted some of the best minds of the Roman world, and most of the educated classes. The Gospel of John, for example, could not be understood by an uneducated person. It presumes knowledge of philosophy. Later on, in further development of the Doctrine of the Resurrection, it was the Trinitarian Formula which captured the minds and hearts of the Roman world. And the essence of this doctrine is the idea of the living Christ and that God is best known through the person of Jesus. This formula gave meaning to the confused world of that period; it conquered all other answers. This is historical fact, yet from a twentieth century point of view, it must seem virtually impossible. Can this be explained adequately? Perhaps not, but we can try.

As has been explained, the Cross, according to Christian doctrine, is a symbol of the triumph of evil over the power of good. If the Cross were the end of the story, one could make a good case for a pessimistic view of life. But the story did not end with this event. The Resurrection meant, and continues to mean that God did not lose, that the Good finally did triumph, that two great powers—evil and death—were overcome. If Jesus was raised up, then this is the one great demonstration by God to mankind that evil is not the dominant force in life, that death is not the final conqueror, that God's power is the most real and enduring, and that God is on the side of goodness. Christianity, therefore, right from the beginning, saw the whole drama of the Resurrection as historical proof that life was meaningful, that it was not ultimately tragic, but finally triumphant. Without this historical event, man could never be sure that the Good did win out, and that life was not meaningless. This event is the one great demonstration of God's love for man, a clear sign of the real nature of life. "Be of good cheer," said Christ, "I have overcome the world" (John 16:33).

It is in the writings of Paul that this point is made crystal clear. For he said that "if Christ be not risen, then *is* our preaching vain, and your faith *is* also vain (I Corinthians

15:14). It is clear that Paul knew full well the consequences here. He knew that if there was no Resurrection then there were no valid reasons for accepting any of the teachings of Jesus. If Jesus was claiming God's authority for His insights, preaching about God's will for man, promising meaning to man, what use is it all if it ends only in a quick death? Indeed, if Jesus had kept silent, He would have lived longer. Does this not make the teachings a mockery? Moreover, if Jesus was just another good man, on what grounds do we accept His teachings rather than some other good man's statements? And why even try for "the good life" if it results in evil and death? If evil wins out, why pretend that it pays to be good? By what authority and standard do we accept the teachings of Christ? If they are not from God, they are not the whole story and it is idolatry to follow one man. These are the full and grim implications of the Cross *without* the Resurrection. They are so grim that few people have dared to face up to them. Yet the majority of people believe that life is good, that it makes sense, that good men like Jesus, Socrates, and Buddha, should be taken seriously. But these same people never really consider *why* all this should be taken seriously. They just *feel* that life is worth living. They do not believe in the Resurrection—this is fantastic; but they do believe, *must* believe that life is worthwhile. What is their evidence? What is their answer to the pessimist? They have no real answer. It is a blind faith. Paul knew this and faced it. That is why he dared to state the case very bluntly: If the Resurrection is not true, *then* "we are most miserable." It means that the pessimist is right. Let's face it. But if the Resurrection is true, *then* "thanks *be* to God, which giveth us the victory through our Lord Jesus Christ" (I Corinthians 15:57).

This is the primary reason why the Doctrine of the Resurrection is such a key tenet in the Christian faith. In a very real sense, there would be no Christianity without it. Historically, this is certainly true. If the Cross had been the last act of Christ, it is quite certain the disciples would never have been heard from again. It is even more certain that the Resurrection was the event which brought them together again, and which led to the founding of the Christian Church. As a matter of historical record, therefore, *it is* the Resurrection which caused the founding of the Christian religion. Whether we ourselves believe the Doctrine of the Risen Christ or not, the fact is that it is the chief cause of the Christian religion.

Let us, then, summarize the chief points of this chapter. In terms of "proof," there is no clear-cut scientific evidence to verify the Doctrine of the Resurrection, nor is there much to deny it. The usual modern scientific arguments against the Resurrection are exactly arguments, not facts. That is to say, we moderns argue that a resurrection hasn't happened to anybody else in history; there are no other similar events to corroborate the Resurrection of Christ. In addition, what we know of natural laws lends weight to disbelief in Christ's Resurrection. These are all perfectly good arguments, but it is essential to recognize that they are only arguments, not data. Furthermore, the arguments do not tell us anything about the Resurrection *per se*. They merely tell us that there is no evidence for *other* resurrections, and, statistically, this Christian Resurrection is unlikely. But any honest scientist would not leap beyond data and statistics and then categorically deny the possibility of the "unlikely" and the unique. As we pointed out in Chapter II, science cannot deal with the unique. If this Resurrection of Christ was unique, then by definition, scientific comparison is at once limited, if not impossible. In other words, for any who accept a scientific criterion as the *sole* method of ascertaining truth, the Resurrection will be viewed with great scepticism and at best a firm agnosticism. But it is a dogma to say that by definition no resurrection of any kind could ever happen. That cannot be proved on any terms by anyone. Thus, within narrow factual data, the Resurrection cannot be demonstrated either as undoubtedly true or inevitably false.

If, on the other hand, one accepts wider categories of truth and validity, then there is more evidence on the side of the Christian story. We have described the experiences of the disciples as recorded in the New Testament, a valid kind of empirical data which any scientist must consider. The difficulty is, of course, that like most personal experiences, the analysis and interpretation can never be wholly objective or complete. But the weight of scholarly evidence seems to leave us with a balance in favor of the validity of the New Testament analysis and interpretation.

We also described the Christian argument for the Resurrection; namely, that if there were no Resurrection, then the authority of Christ is removed, and the general significance of His whole life is one of tragedy and meaninglessness, and so by implication, all of life is tragedy. From a rational point of view, then, the Christian belief in the Resurrection is reasonable and logical. For if Christ were the Incarnation of God, or if He were only a representative claiming true insight for His teachings, then His claim is validated by the unique drama of the Cross and Resurrection. Conversely, if there were no Resurrection, there are no grounds for believing Jesus. For Christians to make the claim that a special revelation occurred in Christ only to have it all defeated, would be highly unreasonable. At the same time, like the scientific problem, this type of reasoning does not prove decisively the Resurrection, either. For the reasoning process here takes place within the larger context of faith, that is, the acceptance of Christ as the God-Man—the bearer of revelation. And this leads to the final point of the chapter.

The Doctrine of the Resurrection, like the Doctrines of Revelation and Incarnation, cannot be fairly evaluated in isolation. The three doctrines are bound together. The Christian argument is that all three stand or fall together, that it is virtually impossible to hold to one without logically retaining the other two. The bare proposition that "Christ rose from the dead" is a fantastic and incredible statement. But if Christ was in some sense a unique revelation of God, if Christ was in some sense God incarnate, then is it not plausible to expect the God in Christ *not* to be killed? If God was present in the whole drama of the life and death of Christ, is God to be defeated at the end? If by the term, we mean Ultimate Reality, how could God be ultimate if evil and death were stronger and won out? If that happened, then evil and death are ultimate—they are the gods, the ruling powers in life. If this were true, then Christianity would be absolutely wrong. Yet it is precisely this possibility that the early Christians had to face and did face. But it was their series of experiences which finally convinced them that God was God and that evil and death were not the gods. Those experiences have been shared by millions of Christians since the New Testament period.

In summary, what these shared experiences mean is this: that the disciples, like other Christians since, when confronted by Christ, believe that they are experiencing God most really, that the God one comes to know through Christ is a living and active God, and that in this sense, at least, the Christ lives on. Because this set of experiences, which have been widely shared, is so different from other types, it seems to point to some kind of unique activity of God. It is significant because the Christian experiences of God in Christ are not retentions of ideas about God. The Christian tradition is not one in which everyone agrees that God is the Prime Mover, or the First Cause, or Abstract Reason, nor is it one of just recalling to mind a noble teacher, a beloved physician. Intellectual concepts do not excite the total person very much, nor do sentimental memories of good men. The whole testimony of the Christian witness is a total experience of the living God as He revealed Himself through Christ, then and ever since. Unless there were something objective in the order of life, something "there" in the stream of history, it is difficult to see how so many Christians could have the same profound and meaningful experience.

In the last analysis, Christianity cannot prove conclusively by any one method the Doctrine of the Resurrection or the Doctrines of Revelation and Incarnation. But taken as a whole, within the context of human experiences of God, these three descriptions make sense. One cannot convince a person by argument that he should accept the doctrines, and one should not insist on complete agreement on details in the descriptions. The only real court of appeals that Christianity can refer to is one's own personal religious experience. It is the Christian faith, therefore, that, if one is acquainted with God in his own experience, however dimly at first, *then* the Christian descriptions will make sense to him, and not before. As we have mentioned previously, this is also true of human love. Romantic descriptions and doctrines of love leave the loveless cold. But when a person is in love he knows what poets mean and is grateful for their help in interpretation. God is more important than theology; it is experiences of God that are of prime importance. If theology, like poetry, can aid us in understanding, explaining, and interpreting these experiences, then theology has served its purpose.

9

DOCTRINE OF THE ATONEMENT

I F THE New Testament story of God's great part in the life, death and resurrection of Jesus is true, the next question is, "Why did God do all this?" The Doctrine of the Atonement is the attempt to answer this query. Like some other doctrines, this one has had a stormy and varied history! It may be admitted that, for most moderns, all of the interpretations are both archaic and meaningless. Such terms as "The Blood of the Lamb," "The Sacrificial Christ," "Died for our Sins," etc., seem crude and barbaric. But the original question is still an important one, and, I believe, the essence of the original answer is also important.

There is a basic problem involved behind the question of the Atonement. This problem is the estrangement of man from God. In the Doctrine of Man, one definition of sin meant man's alienation from God. We stated that man's natural condition always includes sin. Even though man has within himself an image of God, nevertheless, he is still separated from God. Man's spiritual anxiety is the clue to the fact that, though he may long for God, he has not yet found God. In addition, man's pride often leads him to the belief that God is unnecessary. In either case, there is a separation between man and God. The Doctrine of the Atonement is the theological attempt to describe how God took the initiative and sought to overcome man's estrangement.

The four major interpretations of these doctrines are: [1] First, the *Latin* or legalistic description. This view is most clearly set forth by Anselm who said that Christ, by His death, earned an excess of merit. This merit is paid to God as satisfaction or compensation for man's sin. This payment was necessary because man, being sinful, is unable to make the necessary satisfaction. Since man cannot do this, God must do it. Therefore, God became man in Jesus. Christ as the perfect man did what sinful man could not do. If this was the case, then the justice of God is satisfied.

The second interpretation, called the *Sacrificial view,* is not dissimilar from the Latin view. This description, used by the writers of the book of Hebrews, also assumes that man cannot redress his guilt and sin, but that God's justice must be satisfied. What is required, therefore, is a vicarious sacrifice. Jesus, as man, sacrificed Himself for all mankind. He was "the Blood of the Lamb," the sinless and innocent man who died for all men. In this act, God's wrath is appeased, justice maintained, and God's loving relationship to man established.

The third interpretation of the Atonement is called the *Subjective view* which was perhaps best elucidated in the nineteenth century by Schliermacher, Ritschl and Rashdall. These men asserted that since God's attitude towards man was only one of love and never one of wrath, no sacrifice or compensation was required. The meaning of Christ's noble death is that it thereby inspires man to new moral achievements. Man now knows he is "at home in the universe" and can count on God's continuing support and guidance. The effect of Christ's death, therefore, was to provide greater

[1] For a further but succinct discussion of the four interpretations of the Atonement, see Gustaf Aulen, *Christus Victor;* Macmillan, New York, 1931.

stimulus to man's moral endeavors. Atonement means moral uplift.

The fourth view of the Atonement is called the *Classical view*. This can be found in the writings of Paul, Irenaeus, and Luther. According to this interpretation the early Christian answer to "Why did God do all this?" was that "God so loved the world (man), that he gave his only begotten Son, that whosoever believeth in him should not perish, but have everlasting life" (John 3:16). This means that God wanted to show man that life was basically meaningful, that evil and death were not the conquering powers, that the Good was the most real and triumphant, and that life, therefore, was not tragic. Man, in other religions and philosophies, hoped and guessed that life was meaningful; some had partial evidence for this view. But man also was at times pessimistic and, with other partial evidence, felt life was basically evil. Now, according to Christian doctrine, with the drama of Christ, God Himself has taken the initiative and shown man the real nature of life. He has done this not by fiat or terror, but by a great act of love. He has lowered Himself to man's status, assumed the role of a suffering servant, endured the worst ignominies of defeat and death— the ultimate sacrifice and demonstration of love. God came not as a conquering potentate who cowed men into belief, but as a loving servant evoking spontaneous love. From the Christian viewpoint this deed is also a demonstration of the ultimate use of power. If God is all powerful, theoretically, He could force all men into obedience. But not to use power that way, even though He could, reveals the power to restrain power. To have absolute power and then use it in such a way as to evoke the free response of man in love is the ultimate power. And that is why Christianity has always defined God's power as essentially that of love. Atonement, therefore, means literally AT-ONE-MENT—God and man at one

—together. The Doctrine of the Atonement is a description of God's love for man. This is the core of the description and the answer to the original question.

The other interpretations stem from this basic one and were altered slightly to meet other types of questions. For example, one other interpretation of the Doctrine of the Atonement uses legal language. It states that since man was so sinful, he could not possibly make up for his errors. This meant that the wrath and justice of God could not be appeased. But Christ did what man could not do—He, being without sin, took on the burden of all man's sins and sacrificed Himself for man. He thereby appeased God and man is forgiven by Christ's deed. Christ atoned for, made up for our sins. Note that "atone" here means not so much togetherness, as redress, or making up for mistakes and sins. This kind of description bothers most of us today because it seems very legal and very harsh. Also, it seems to picture God as a tyrannical despot, a capricious and loveless judge. On the other hand, if one were a Christian in the earlier days of Christianity and were trying to explain the significance of the Atonement, and if his audience were a lawyer or a group of people trained in a legalistic religion, then one would probably use this type of argument. And, of course, that is precisely what happened. Paul used this type of description when explaining the Atonement to law-minded Romans, and legalistic Jews. On the other hand, when Paul or John were talking to someone else with a different cultural background, they used other interpretations.

Thus, if we take any of the interpretations of the Atonement out of their cultural context, if we take them literally, and as being complete authoritative descriptions for all time, we will both falsify them on the one hand, and make nonsense out of them on the other hand. The common denominator behind all the crude and archaic words is "togetherness"—God's great act of love towards mankind. This is the real essence of the Doctrine of the Atonement. And again, this doctrine is not primarily an argument *for* Christianity. It is not a method of proving anything. It is foremost an attempted answer to the question, "Why did God reveal Himself and incarnate Himself through Christ? Why the Cross and Resurrection?" The Doctrine of the Atonement is Christanity's answer to this problem. Not to answer it is irresponsibility. The answer will not, by itself, mean anything to anybody. But with the other Christian doctrines, it fits reasonably well, is consistent with the Christian view of the Nature of God, and represents at the least, Christianity's attempt to be honest and provide rational descriptions.

10

ETERNAL LIFE

ONE of man's most persistent and age-old questions has been, "Is there life after death?" Christianity is not unique in believing that there is some kind of after-life. The majority of the world's religions, primitive and sophisticated, hold some view of life after death. But not all views are the same. One of the chief difficulties with the Christian description of eternal life is that most of it is negative. That is to say, Christian theologians spend considerable time trying to make clear what they do *not* believe about immortality. This is necessary in order to distinguish the Christian view from other descriptions. For example, strictly speaking, Christianity does not believe in immortality in the Platonic sense of the word. Christianity does *not* believe that man, after death, is raised up and absorbed into some divine mind. We do not believe that the body and soul are two absolutely distinct entities which are separated at death. Immortality in much of Greek philosophy usually means that the soul or mind is thus freed from the body and is then united with the divine soul or mind of the universe. Immortality, for Plotinus, for example, means absorption into the divine mind or, for Plato, man achieves the role of a thinking spectator above and beyond the earthly life.

Similarly, Christianity does not agree with some of the Oriental views of immortality, such as that of Hinduism, for these views, generally, adopt an absorption theory. In Hinduism, for example, man, after death, is viewed as becoming one with God, being completely absorbed into God. There may be many intermediary stages of birth and rebirth, but ultimately the goal is union with the divine, however that may be defined. The chief disagreement between these views and the Christian view is the problem of individuality. This is also the basic difference between Greek and Christian views. In other words, most all non-Christian views of immortality involve the loss of the individual person. Each person is lost in the divine; he becomes merely one atom like all other atoms. There is nothing to distinguish him from anyone else, nor even from God.

By contrast, Christianity believes that whatever eternal life means, it involves retaining the individual, unique personality. If this is not true, then after-life has no special meaning or significance to the Christian. If the unique individual is lost in immortality, even lost in God, then for Christianity there is no real life after death. When the unique person is dead, he is dead. Any idea that our remains, bodily or spiritual, will be raised up and amalgamated into some divine stuff or power is meaningless and hopeless for the Christian. Thus, in a negative way, Christianity finally gets around to its first positive assertion about life after death.

Eternal life means first of all, then, that the unique personality of a person never dies; it lives forever—hence, eternal life. This basic conviction has been variously described in Christian theology. In Paul, at first glance, it looks as though there is a straight body-spirit dualism. But on more careful reading, especially of I Corinthians 15, it is quite clear that Paul is not guilty of a dualism at all, for he speaks of "the corruptible body" being "raised up incorruptible," and of the fact that "we are changed." This represents Paul's attempt to avoid the idea that only some kind of a "spirit" is resurrected. He is trying to say that some kind of "changed, incorruptible" entity ("body") is raised up. This type of description would correspond to what Paul knew about the resurrection appearances of Christ. At the same time, he knows he cannot be precise and detailed; this is a fundamental mystery, as he says in so many words. Yet it is reasonably clear that Paul is affirming his belief that the individual person will always retain his individuality and uniqueness in life after death. The word "fellowship" with God also implies a personal existence, for one does not have fellowship with a tree, or a group of spiritual atoms, but only with a "fellow," a personality. This, then, is the basic affirmation of Christianity, that eternal life means the survival of the unique personality after death, and an existence in fellowship with God.

At this point, we become modern again and ask, "How does Christianity know this; what is the evidence?" Christianity would first reply by admitting there is no concrete, scientific evidence for eternal life. No human being has come back from the grave and beyond to report to us, or show us movies. This is why Christianity cannot subscribe to some of the primitive descriptions of heaven and/or hell. Or, as Reinhold Niebuhr put it, "We cannot describe the furniture of heaven nor the temperature of hell." [1] Further, there is no biological evidence. Indeed, quite the contrary. We know that our physical bodies decay and disintegrate in the grave. Thus, to put it very crudely, we know that we will not have to clean our fingernails in life after death! We have no physical, chemical or reliable psychological evidence of eternal life. And given our descriptions of the methods and tools of these branches of science, there is no reason why we should have any such evidence. By definition, these enterprises are

[1] *Discerning the Signs of the Times;* Scribners, New York, 1946: p. 154.

limited and concerned with *this* life. There is no way in which the tools could be applied to this problem. So it should be obvious that there is no scientific evidence for eternal life and Christianity would look with suspicion on anyone who claimed he did have this kind of evidence.

There are other types of evidences. First is the evidence of the resurrected Christ. It is obvious that Paul, in addition to his own experience on the Damascus Road, used the evidences of the Resurrection as his foundation for belief in eternal life. This, of course, is true for the disciples, apostles, and most later Christians. If the Resurrection is accepted, then it gives authority to the teachings of Jesus which also make clear the idea of eternal life. But the Resurrection of Christ alone, even if indisputably true, would not necessarily mean that life after death was open to us. For if Christ were the Son of God, then we might well expect *Him* to be raised up. But since we are only ordinary mortals, what hope is there for us? The answer to this problem is that the teachings of Jesus specifically promised mankind eternal life, directly and indirectly. "Seek the Kingdom of God first," "Great will be your reward in heaven," "I go to prepare a place for you," "If I be lifted up, I will raise all men unto me." Thus, the Resurrection of Christ supports His teachings. Of course, this argument does not prove eternal life, but it does offer consistency, unity, and integrity between the act and the teachings. This suggests, therefore, a certain correspondence between experience and interpretation. And if one accepts the whole drama of the Cross and the Resurrection as being a series of objective events, then considerable weight must be given to the teachings of Jesus, which preceded the events.

The Gospel of John suggests another type of evidence. One of the chief messages of this Fourth Gospel is the proclamation that eternal life can be partly realized and lived now, on this earth. If it is true that fellowship with God is part of the nature of life after death, then one can experience some of that now. For, the whole point of Jesus' teachings was to enable man to have fellowship with God, now. Man can and does experience God in *this* life. We can have a genuine relationship with God now. If this is true, then we already experience something of life everlasting. The key to this description of John's is that eternal life (heaven) is *not* so much a *place,* but a *quality* of living. Similarly, hell is not a place down in the middle of the earth; it, too, is a quality of existence. The great insight, therefore, which the Fourth Gospel offers us, is the suggestion that eternal life is a quality of life, a superior type of living which has both a timeless and a spaceless aspect to it.

This insight is not so fantastic as it might first appear, for it can be partially verified by our everyday experience. When we use the slang expression, "I went through hell last week," what we mean is that our life in the past week was very difficult, anxious, and unhappy. Conversely, when we say, "I had a heavenly time," we mean that the quality of existence in a given period was easier, more secure, and happier. Or, take another example which points up our awareness of time and space. When we are in great pain and suffering, we are very conscious of both time and space. On a hospital bed of pain, we constantly say to ourselves, "When will I get out of this place (space)?" *"When* (time) will this pain subside?" Hell might be defined as an extreme consciousness of and unhappiness in time and space. Hell is thus a quality of living.

On the other hand, we also have experiences in which we are relatively unaware of time and space. Moments or adventures in which we find ourselves exceedingly joyful and happy have a kind of timelessness about them. This is realized when someone suddenly interrupts us and says, "Hurry, it is almost time for supper." We then look at our watch and exclaim, "Why, so it is. I wasn't *aware of the time*. Where has the afternoon gone?" Similarly, the experiences of a happily married couple give another clue to a character of living which comes close to what we mean by eternal life. A couple, profoundly in love, married, say, for five or ten years, will often say that it seems to them as if they had always been married. Even the romantic little ditty that "I only began to live when I married you," reflects the same idea. In both religious and psychological histories of conversion and integration, people speak of being "born again" or "I feel like a new man." Thus, there seems to be an abundant number of human experiences which give us the feeling that time and space are not very important, that there is a kind of living which seems endless or timeless—eternal.

Thus, the Christian view of eternal life is not radically different from known types of human experience. The relationship we have with God in this life is essentially the same as that which we shall have in the life to come, with the addition that the fellowship is more intense and complete. Presumably, also, the love and friendship we experience here with our family or intimate friends is more perfectly realized in the hereafter. If this is true, then it is also clear that the real basis of all of this is the power of love—human and divine. It is experiences of love which can make life heavenly, and lack of love which can make it hellish. We have noted that one of the Christian definitions of Reality (God) is that of love. Eternal life, therefore, is realizing the love of God. When this is done, the particular time we die and the place where we are buried seem very insignificant. It is but a fleeting moment within a process of endless moments, a flickering time that marks the renewal of what we have already experienced, the completion of the purpose of life itself.

This, then, is the chief, positive assertion of Christianity about the nature of eternal life. There are many unanswered questions left and in our opinion they will always be a mystery for us in this life. Problems of *where* we go in the life hereafter, labels like "up" or "down," when and how, are basically unanswerable. Such questions also reflect our bondage to ordinary concepts of time and space. Ordinary ideas of space and time, by definition, cannot apply to something that is without time and space. Thus, Christianity would say we are faced with mystery here, and it is folly to pretend we have an answer. Our categories are simply inadequate.

Similarly, the whole problem of the Last Judgment remains obscure. The vivid pictures in art and theology of various courtroom scenes, the throne of God, the Advocate, and the like, make no sense to us if taken in any literal sense. The primary purpose behind descriptions of the Last Judgment is the problem of justice in life. Since evil does sometimes win out in this life, the good are often defeated; some ultimate defeat of evil is essential if we believe in the Resurrection and the supremacy of God's moral order. Presumably, therefore, the good triumphs at the last, if not before. What this means precisely in terms of timeless and the spaceless, we do not know. Hence, confusion and vagueness are caused by attempts to reduce the problem to our ideas of time and space. Christianity believes in some kind of judgment as being necessary to vindicate the moral structure of life. But how this occurs, and what the full implications involve, we do not know. Furthermore, we also believe that judgment is not merely a legal procedure, but is tempered by the love of God. This means that our standards of love and justice probably fall far short of God's criterion. For this reason, hasty statements about damnation and salvation must be viewed with suspicion. Some theologians, both Roman Catholic and Protestant, assume too much knowledge about whom God "damns" or "saves." The fact is we do not know and can never know in this life.

We could go on describing the various arguments about these problems, and there are other problems involved in eternal life that are equally puzzling. But it is neither the purpose nor the scope of this book to recite the historical pros and cons of all possible problems. We have tried to describe the essence of the Christian belief in eternal life and beyond this we must, like Paul, admit our ignorance. "We know only in part," and have tried to say what we know and believe. "Now we see through a glass darkly; but then face to face," and *then* we shall "know fully" (I Corinthians 13:12).

The Christian Doctrine of Eternal Life, like the other doctrines, is a product of experience, interpretation, faith, reason. This particular doctrine is especially filled with mystery which makes clear-cut proofs or disproofs on either side impossible. But again, we believe it is an essential part of the Christian faith and that it harmonizes with the rest of Christian experience.

11

THE CHRISTIAN INTERPRETATION
OF HISTORY

I N THE previous chapters, some points of the description have led to statements about the meaning of history—for example, that God is the Lord of history, that the historical process is a moral one, and that history has meaning and purpose. It remains, therefore, for us to make more explicit the Christian view of history. The problem of whether history has an order to it, whether it has a meaning, and whether it is "going somewhere," was a neglected concern for most Americans until recently. Now that we have participated in two great world wars and are faced with enormous world-wide problems, we have become more conscious of both the world-at-large and the problem of history itself. It is perhaps no accident that the threat of destruction or defeat in the world wars and the threat of possible annihilation in the event of a future war, has raised the question of "What is history all about?" This, too, perhaps answers the questions as to why various books on the nature of history have become so popular. Toynbee's monumental work, *A Study of History,* was written in the 1930's, but the one volume condensation was a best-seller in the late 1940's. Scholars and laymen alike are now very much interested in the problem of meaning in history.

Christianity has had an interpretation of history that has remained fairly consistent since its derivation from Judaism. The general over-all historical view of Christianity runs something like this. In the beginning was God—the original and Ultimate Reality and Power. God then created the galaxy of stars, gases, and worlds, followed by the natural process in which "the spark of life" and cellular life appeared, and finally, natural laws of birth, growth, decay, gravity, etc. This process is the story of evolution which the scientists can best describe to us. All that Christianity says is that the original source and beginning was God. From that point on, evolution works according to inherent natural laws. Eventually, human life appeared, when and how, we do not know. (As noted previously, the Adam and Eve story is not a scientific treatise on the origin of man, but is primarily a religious myth about the origin of evil in human nature.)

After the gradual evolution of man is the beginning of what is called *human* history. The period from the earliest, primitive man through primitive religion, through higher religions to Judaism represents man's growth and search for meaning in his life. According to the Christian view, the birth of Judaism under Moses marks a significant growth in man's history. This is called "the preparation stage" of history. This means that Judaism was preparing the world for the Incarnation. Christianity sees Judaism as pointing to the Messiah. The whole history of the Jewish religion is one of great expectation. God, through the prophets, in diverse ways, seemed to be saying to man that He would reveal Himself. Prior to Judaism, man was reaching up towards God, seeking reality, truth, and meaning. The great religions of the Orient, and the philosophy of the Greeks portray the heights of human aspiration and reach. Now, with the advent of Judaism, God responds to man's search by declaring that He would give man further knowledge of life. More important, since God has always sought man's loving response, God demonstrated clearly His own love for man by giving Himself to man. Thus, when Jesus appeared, God Incarnate appeared, in human history. The life and teachings of Jesus, the whole drama of the Cross and Resurrection are the fulfillment of God's promise to Judaism and mankind. Thus, for Christianity, Christ is the center of history. This is the point where truth is given to man. If this is so, then we are able to see backwards in history and thereby understand something about the origin and growth of history. And we can also look forward in history and know something about its future and ultimate end. Christ, therefore, is the key to the understanding of history.

The Christian view of history from the period of Christ until the present day is that the process is a gradual realization of God's sovereignty, or fulfillment of the Kingdom of God. Indeed, this is the course until the end of history. Christianity would say, therefore, that the historical process from Christ to the end of history is an "interim period." It is the interim between the revelation of what the true nature and purpose of life is *and* its fulfillment. That is to say, we know about the nature of good and evil, the purpose of love, and the reason for living, but the triumph of love and justice will not be complete until the end of history. The end of history means the fulfillment of God's purpose, and the final establishment of His Kingdom. What is *beyond* the end of history, what the "establishment of the Kingdom" means is very similar to the problem of Eternal Life. We can offer no details, nor imagine any spatial kingdom somewhere. It is another basic mystery. Such is the general outline of the Christian view of history.

It is certainly obvious that such a sketchy outline passes over a multitude of questions and problems. Within the scope of this book, all the detailed problems cannot be treated fairly. But it is necessary to examine the chief issues.

The first problem concerning the nature of history is whether there is a moral order in the process. This is the great contribution of Judaism, particularly the prophets. The Hebrew prophets emphasized above all that the structure of history is basically a moral one. Therefore, obedience to this moral order, created and maintained by God, was the first duty of men and nations. Christianity adopts this insight also. Thus, Judaism and Christianity are alike in their conviction that just as there are laws in nature, there are moral laws imbedded in the structure of history. This is an orderly and lawful universe. If man disobeys the laws of nature or of mental health, trouble follows. Similarly, it is the Judeo-Christian faith, that if man disobeys the moral law, trouble follows.

What does this belief mean in detail? The prophets gave crystal clear applications. To them it meant that general laws of justice, equality, love, service, and neighborliness, were not just subjective ideas of people, but that these attitudes and relationships are part of the very structure of life. The nature of reality is akin to these qualities; it supports and fosters these relationships. Therefore, if mankind is to improve, he must discover these laws and seek to abide by them. This means that nations must try to realize these laws in their enonomic, political, and social policies. If they do not, they will not long endure. The prophets reiterated this theme over and over again. Today, Christianity still holds to this basic theme.

In terms of social causation, it does not mean that economic and political policies are unimportant. Economic policies do cause various events. But Christianity would say that social policies reflect the moral or immoral motives and attitudes of the people. In this sense, social and political policies are *results* of personal and group motives and morals. The primary causes of historical behavior are moral. All our concerns and interests spring from our inner motivations, and these desires and wants express themselves through economic and political measures. This is why Christianity cannot accept as adequate most secular views of history. Christianity cannot agree that history is almost entirely determined by economic factors, as both the fathers of Communism (Marx and Engels) and Capitalism (Harrington, Ricardo, and Locke among others) asserted. Nor can Christianity agree with the views which say that the sole determining causes are political policies, or psychological, or geographical, or glandular characteristics. In reply to these various views, we would say that obviously all these aspects are causes of the historical process, but that no *one* set of influences is the determining cause. We believe history is much more complicated than that. As we analyze history, we believe we can find situations in which, say, the economic factors were predominant, but in another period, the political or psychological aspects seemed to dominate. Indeed, the recent trend among contemporary historians seems to reject all simple notions of single causation in history.[1] If these historians are right, however, it would seem to invalidate the Christian view, which asserts the primacy of the moral cause.

On the other hand, Christianity does not hold to a simple moral theory of causation. It is true, as has been stated, that, according to Christian doctrine, it is the inner motivation of people which largely determines their economic and political behavior. On the other hand, it is equally true that economic and political policies and conditions directly *affect* one's motivation, responses, and attitudes. There is, therefore, an interaction between motives and external conditions. To the Christian way of thinking, this is what complicates historical analysis. For we can never be sure how much events are determined by the interests of people, or how much prior events determine the interests of these same people. We are

[1] See especially R. H. MacIver, *Social Causation;* Ginn, New York, 1942.

sure that there is mutual effect, but how to plot precisely the various shifts and nuances is one of the basic complexities facing any analyst.

It should also be pointed out that when Christianity asserts the moral process to be the basis of history, it is *not* saying that all people act from moral motives. What we mean here is that we believe that the order of history is a moral order, as the order of nature is a lawful one. However, like natural law, we do not know all the laws. There is no simple definition of moral processes in historical events. We believe there is a basic moral structure to life, but how it operates in this and that event we are not sure. This is why Christian theologians speak of the "hidden" justice of God. But from what we do know of the moral order of history we believe it tends to support relationships of justice and love. This moral order, like natural order, is objective; it is "out there" in life. But this is different from implying that all men act from "good motives." We are quite sure men do not. The point is, however, that whatever our motives, they tend to produce social arrangements according to our likes and dislikes. The problem, as Christianity sees it, is whether what we like is what the moral order likes. If our plans are contrary to the structure of morality, then Christianity would say that trouble lies ahead. On the other hand, if our schemes are approaching the moral order, the chances are better that less trouble will occur. Moral cause, therefore, in the Christian view, means that there are general moral laws in the structure of history and these laws cannot be permanently defied. It is the Christian faith that continual defiance of morality inevitably results in disaster. Thus, the causes of historical events are a complicated and varying set of psychological, economic and political factors. But whether these influences produce security and creativity, or insecurity and disaster, depends upon whether or not this amalgam of influences approaches the moral order. Man thus has freedom to choose all kinds of policies, but he is not free to escape either the good or bad results of the decisions. Similarly, we would say man is free to ignore the laws of physical and mental health, but if he continues to ignore them he cannot escape disease and illness. Note that the inner motives of such a man are the direct cause of his actions.

There is also an objective and lawful structure to life which cannot be ignored without harm. Therefore, it may be said that man is a cause in history, but the ultimate effects are largely determined by law. In other words, history has its laws and these are finally determinative. In this sense, Christianity asserts God's righteous, moral order to be the cause of history. This is why the Hebrew prophets and later Christian prophets could predict the fall of certain great nations. These nations had become so corrupt that they were "an offense against the moral order." Therefore, they were doomed. The limits of such prophecy can be seen in that few prophets, if any, can say precisely when a corrupt nation will fall. Thus, a Christian historian would agree with most secular historians in analyzing the many economic and social policies which led to decay and downfall. But the Christian would go on to examine the moral or immoral motives of the nation which partly produced the disastrous policies. When and if such can be found, the Christian would see here a partial vindication of his interpretation of history.

A. *The Problem of Evil*

The second great problem involved in any view of history is the problem of good and evil. We have already made some general remarks on this subject. Before proceeding, however, let us define our terms. For our purposes here, "good" means whatever factors in history tend to promote creative life;

"evil" means whatever factors tend to destroy life. It is obvious that history is a vast mixture of good and evil. For a Christian who believes in a "good God," and the moral order of history, the problem of evil is an acute one. The perennial question always arises, "If God is good and also powerful, how can He allow such ghastly wars and disease?" By contrast, the Stoic who does not hold to belief in a good God has an easier answer. His answer is that there isn't any real solution to the problem of evil; one can only accept the mixture of good and evil life offers. And one's solace is that most people receive a tolerable share of each; indeed, just enough good to make life worth-while. Within the context of Stoicism this is a respectable and noble answer. But one cannot accept this answer within Christianity and still have integrity. The problem of evil is perhaps the most difficult one for Christianity, yet it is also the stumbling block for most other religions and philosophies, too. What does Christianity say?

First of all, it admits the fundamental character of mystery. This is to say, we have some answers to the problem, but we do not have all the answers, and we are suspicious of anyone who claims he has a simple answer. However, Christian doctrine does offer some explanations.

There are two major kinds of evil: natural evil and human evil. Natural evil is seen in earthquakes, famines and diseases. These are evil from our human point of view because they tend to destroy human life. The question then is, why is there this type of evil? The Christian answer is that since the natural process is a created one, it is not perfect. It is a dynamic process that is imperfect and is perhaps on its way to some type of perfection. Meanwhile, since it is not yet perfect, these aberrations occur. On the other hand, science tells us that some of these "mistakes of nature" are not "bad miracles," but are events which are quite understandable; that is, they are the results of known natural laws.

Furthermore, some diseases and most famines can be either cured or prevented. The tree that falls on a person we may regard as a "natural evil." On the other hand, given the wind and the rotted roots, the tree *had* to fall—by natural law of cause and effect. That a person happened to be under the tree at that precise moment is accidental. Natural evil, therefore, in the Christian view, is not all evil; much of it is accidental. What we mean here is that nature *per se* is not evil. Nature is essentially good and it acts in accordance with its established laws. But some of the effects of natural events *accidentally* harm humans and in that sense only is it evil. As to why this person and not that person gets hurt by the tree, why this child gets this incurable disease and not that one, we do not know. This is the accidental and mysterious part of natural evil. We do not know. And we *emphatically reject* the answer which says that such accidents are punishment for sin. It is preposterous to say that a baby born a Mongoloid idiot must have sinned in his mother's womb and is thereby doomed to such a terrible if brief existence. And it is equally unjust to say that God is punishing the parents by taking it out on the child. Christianity does not believe in that kind of God.

Christianity, therefore, would say that much of natural evil appears to be destructive, but not as much as we think. For we can do a great deal to prevent many accidents. Nevertheless, some evil, so far as we can see, does exist. And this, we believe, is accidental and the result of an imperfect natural process. As to the question, why didn't God create a perfect process and so eliminate even the accidental evil, the answer is we do not know. This is an unanswerable question. Why wasn't life created some other way? Nobody knows. Our job is to find out how it was created, what it is like, and then adjust ourselves to it.

The other type of evil is human evil. Christianity is much

more concerned about this type. Human evil, according to Christianity, is a product of man's freedom. Within the limits of nature and social environment, man has freedom to make decisions and to express himself. He is free to seek or reject morality and religion, or social order and political arrangements. Christianity would say, therefore, that much of evil in life is caused by human beings—man's inhumanity to man. In a word, man's sin is the chief cause of evil. The extreme forms of human evil are those barbarous acts of murder, torture, and slavery, particularly when motivated by crude self-interest, hate, and sadistic desire.

But most human evil is more subtle both in motivation and expression. Most evil in life is not directly willed as such by individuals and groups. As Christianity sees it, destruction in life is caused by a thousand everyday decisions of self-interest and ignorance which build up gradually into an obvious crisis. For example, each of us votes on various economic and political policies. We tend to vote in favor of those measures which will benefit us. It is very difficult for us to see how our decisions will turn out in terms of long-range justice and over-all equity. A particular tariff law is a case in point. If we are living in a town whose principal industry is leather goods or toys, we know that the livelihood of our community depends upon the prosperity of the industry. However, a measure before Congress proposes to lower the tariff rate on European leather goods and toys. This is essential, it is argued, if Europe is to get back on its feet economically and withstand Communist pressure. We can understand this argument. But we also know that if the bill is passed it will hurt our industry severely, and, therefore, our town. This is a complicated problem of economics and ethics. We would probably vote against the tariff measure because we know our own town, and our self-interest is more immediately involved. The European problem is farther away, vague, long range, and the issue of self-interest not as imperative. Thus, there is no particularly evil will involved here, no scheming devil operating. But the fact is that a difficult decision such as this, added to thousands of other similar decisions, often leads inevitably to a world crisis. It is the difficult, daily decisions of people which snowball into creative or destructive large scale situations.

In between the crude expressions of destructivity and those of ignorance and understandable self-interest, are actions of national pride and arrogance. As a group, we often do things we would seldom do as individuals. In the past we have ignored the needs of other smaller nations. We have indeed exploited them and enslaved them economically. While individuals have also done this to other individuals, it has hardly been justified as a patriotic duty and as "sound, practical economics."

Christianity, therefore, believes that human beings are responsible for most of the damage done to other human beings. One way or another, we violate the moral law of history by our economic, political and social policies. This disobedience results in the disasters which befall us. This is why Christianity says that God does not cause wars; humanity does. And the answer to the question, "Why does God permit man to destroy man?" is this: Given man's freedom and given the moral order to history, how could God prevent these disasters? The answer would have to be that God could prevent wars only by destroying man's freedom and by upsetting the moral order. Or, we could put it this way: If man could rob, lie, cheat, murder, exploit, and get away with it, what would this show us about life? It would show us that there is no moral law, no God of righteousness. If I could exploit and destroy at will and at the same time achieve peace and prosperity, would it not pay to do this? Would it not indicate that the structure of life supports injustice? And would it not prove that justice and love are futile and powerless? Thus, Christianity turns the question around by saying that given man's sin and destructive actions, if there were no wars and crises, there would be no God, no morality. This is why the Judeo-Christian tradition has always regarded war and calamity as a kind of judgment upon man and a vindication of the moral structure.

The difficulty most of us have with this view is that we tend to personalize it and equate judgment with a capricious God. This is our mistake. The Bible makes it quite clear that the moral structure of history is objective and impersonal. "The rain falls on the just and the unjust," "God is Lord of all," and "there is none beside Him." It is naive to imagine that God is spying on individuals, that He sights one of us making a mistake and then says, "Aha, I shall give him cancer, or make him lose his shirt in the stock market!" Moral justice operates the same way as the laws of nature. It is significant that nobody who is foolish enough to break some natural law, accuses Nature of "picking on him." If a man says he does not believe in the law of gravity, if he says it is a subjective idea of some scientist, and that he will prove it by walking off the top of a building without falling, we know what will happen. When he falls to the ground and is hurt or killed, none of us would personalize nature and say that "*she* unjustly caused this man to be hurt." On the contrary, we would say that the man disobeyed a natural law— "the man asked for it, and got it." Similarly, man is responsible for his own social disasters.

It should be noted, at this point, that the Incarnation raises a difficult problem with regard to the idea of good and evil. If Christ was in some sense the revelation of God, if Christ disclosed some new truth about the nature of God, then this raises the question of the truth about the Good.

For example, does this mean that there was no good and evil before Christ? Obviously, the problem of good and evil was present long before the time of Jesus. One Christian view is that with the coming of Christ, the full truth about the Good was revealed and that from this point on, history is moving towards its great climax—the fulfillment of the Kingdom of God. This means that before Christ man was struggling with the problems of progress, with religions and moralities which sought to define and achieve the good life. But from a Christian point of view, primitive man, say, was neither very good nor very bad. He did not know enough about life to create many great things, nor to destroy very much. Since man did not know Reality (God) very clearly, he could not be held responsible for most of his ignorance. His progress on all lines was slow and gradual. In the primitive and early stages in the historical process, then, Christianity would say that this was a time of relative moral innocence. Man was almost amoral—neither very good nor very bad.

With the rise of higher religions and philosophies, man came to know more about Reality (God) and morality. Man thus was a little more responsible for both his noble deeds and his corrupt ones. With a few exceptions, however, such as the founders of these religions, the broad masses of people were still relatively innocent. They were advanced certainly above primitive man, but from the New Testament standard, still far short.

With the beginning of the Hebrew religion, the preparation stage of history, a new development appears. Yet it is interesting to observe that the Old Testament starts its moral history at an extremely primitive level. In a sense, therefore, the history of Israel mirrors the history of man. It starts with small, nomadic tribes with very crude tribal morality. The Old Testament is the record of the growth from this primitive beginning to new heights of prophetic insight and expectation of the Messiah. From Christianity's view, therefore, Judaism, in this context, might be viewed as a kind of summary of thousands of years of human history condensed into one example. A parallel analogy would be the growth of any one person from birth to maturity. In a very real sense, each of us reflects the history of the human race. As infants, we begin by doing nothing but eating, sleeping, and crying! We are certainly morally innocent in the crib. Then we go through the initial struggle for existence—our problems and wants are fairly simple. Later, our world enlarges, we conflict with other persons, knowledge expands, responsibility enlarges, and our moral sense grows from crude egotism to more refined types. Thus, Christianity sees Judaism as a kind of special replica of human history, but also as a mirror in which is seen the prophetic revelations of the coming of the new Revelation in Christ.

Then, with the Incarnation, God reveals to man the basic nature of Himself and of life. This is the disclosure of *the Good*. Therefore, from this point on, the struggle between good and evil is out in the open, so to speak. Man now knows what good and evil are, and the course of history from this point on is the open battle between good and evil. In the Cross and Resurrection, God showed us the final outcome—the triumph of the Good. But meanwhile, the conflict goes on.

Because there is such a conflict, this means that Christianity sees no easy doctrine of gradual progress in history. It means that Christianity sees history as the growth of more good but also the growth of more evil. This is the paradoxical nature of history. With every new creative achievement comes the possibility of a new destructive situation. To put it mildly, the development of atomic science represents, on the one hand, an enormous creative possibility; on the other hand, it also means a gigantic destructive possibility. The two cannot be separated. Or, in human terms, the more moral a man becomes, the worse he may sin. That is to say, a man with great spiritual and moral character may fall much further morally than a weaker person. The moral giant knows better, and, if he fails, he is responsible. For example, an ignorant tenant farmer who has anti-Negro prejudices, is only relatively immoral in his hatred of Negroes. But a doctor who knows the facts about "races" is much more guilty if he, too, displays anti-Negro attitudes. The doctor knows better; the farmer does not.

Thus, as Christianity sees the historical process, both good and evil are increasing and will continue to expand. This does not mean a simultaneous development, however. We have our ups and downs. Our concern for other people, for justice among nations, improves, but then our wars get bigger and more destructive. There is no automatic pendulum in the Christian view. We are always faced with the possibility of a new destructive period, or a new creative level. We may not reach one or the other; or we may achieve one and not the other. It is not inevitable that both must always occur. We may foresee a danger in time and take steps to avoid it, or we may not see the opportunity for a new level of growth and so miss it. This is what Toynbee means by "the challenge and response" situation. But Christian theology cannot accept easy predictions about challenges and responses in terms of names, dates, and places. Our point is that we do not regard history as a mechanistic cycle of good and evil events, nor do we see history as either a simple line of progress or a straight line leading down to doom and destruction. Thus, we believe that both good and evil continue to grow, and believe that we vacillate somewhere between the extremes of good and evil, and will continue to do so until the end of history.

At this point, one might well ask what does this theory have to do with living now? To answer the question fully would require another book. But we can supply one example which perhaps will give the clue. Let us apply this Christian view of history to the present international situation. Since I cannot predict the future and for the purpose of illustration in this book, I am assuming that the situation will not radically change for several years. We are in a stage of history which has seen two world wars and the threat of a third world war in the space of fifty years. Add to this all the terrible upheavals that result from war, and one has a pretty gloomy picture of modern history. Our immediate worry is whether we will have a third world war. Our greatest fear is that if we do, most of Western civilization, along with untold millions of lives, will be destroyed. It would be very easy to analyze all the forces present in this situation and come to the conclusion that war was inevitable. We could say that there always have been wars in history and therefore there always will be. It is just a question of time. To those who say that war is not inevitable, we could answer by asking for the evidence, and by saying that this is wishful thinking. Most answers which claim to solve the Russian-American tension are notoriously naive. In addition, for the sake of argument, suppose that by a rigorous rational analysis we came to the conclusion that a full-scale war, rather than local, minor aggressions, between America and Russia was a logical necessity. The only question unanswered is, when? What would Christianity say to this? I believe Christianity would say: The Christian view of history is not mechanical. That is to say, nothing is inevitable, and the historical process does not operate according to the narrow confines of human logic. Historical events are enormously complex and while there are laws of cause and effect in operation, there are many complex causes mixed together. All of which makes it difficult for any of us to decipher *which* set of causes are dominant—*here? there?* Can we plot the changes and balances? Christianity would say that no one can fathom the present maze of forces to warrant accurate prediction of future events. In addition, Christianity believes that God is the Lord of History, an active God, which means that new and creative possibilities can occur, new levels of solutions which we could not possibly foresee. What does this mean for us today?

It means that although a rational analysis of the present situation might lead us to the pessimistic conclusion that war is inevitable, Christianity could not accept this as the final truth. Even if all the facts should tell us that it is folly to keep the door open to Russia, useless to have further conferences, and that war is sure to come within three to twelve months, Christianity could not agree wholeheartedly. Why? Because we believe that the human mind cannot possibly foresee all future situations, because we want to leave room for new and unforeseen developments, and because God, through some event or persons, may open a new way. On the other hand, there is no guarantee in the Christian view that this new creation will occur. The gloomy analyst *might* be right. All we are saying is that either turn might occur or a third way open up. Therefore, keep the doors open. In terms of general policy, this does not mean appeasement of Russia, or sitting around doing nothing and waiting for "God to do something." It simply means that we do not close up any possibility for some answer or partial answer. This means that our view of history is not altogether a deterministic one, that there is a spontaneous character to the process which we cannot always predict.

It may be that Western civilization has so continually violated the moral order to history that we are doomed beyond repair. On the other hand, we may respond to the judgments of the last fifty years in such a way as to escape disaster. We have been chastened, Christianity would say, by the moral law operating through historical events. If we are responding morally to this "challenge," we may survive. None of us can tell the depth of our moral conversion. For this reason, we are not sure of our fate *vis-a-vis Russia*. The Christain view, therefore, is neither a simple pessimism nor a simple optimism, but it is a view which we believe is able to face grim realities, yet also retain possibilities for new creative action.

There are two other main problems contained in the Christian interpretation of history. One is the age-old question of the suffering of the innocent. We have tried to explain the sources of evil in life and have described natural and human evil. But this does not answer the question, "Why must the innocent suffer?" So far as I can see, no one has improved Job's answer. All the so-called improvements seem to me to be either an insult to God or an offense to human intelligence. The variety of modern answers from the one which says that pain is an unreal illusion, to the answer that suffering is payment for sin, seem to me to be patently false. Job's answer, of course, is that there is no intellectual answer. This seems to me to be the only honest one. We can figure out, in most instances, the cause of a person's pain and suffering. The suffering of thousands of innocent women and children in the war is caused by human beings. The suffering of a child racked with disease is caused by a virus; that is, by nature. But these explanations do not tell us *why* this group of people or *that* child should suffer, or why the rest of us escape such calamity. This is one of the tragic mysteries of life, and it seems to me that it is only honest to acknowledge this mystery and confess our ignorance. This was what Job concluded. Possibly there is a hint of something further in Job's conclusions. One might interpret Job's "conversation with God" this way. God made a proposition to Job:

"Would you rather have the intellectual answer to this problem *or* the power to endure suffering?" And Job took the latter. All who have experienced great suffering, I rather think, would agree with Job.

In terms of history, the problem is also a baffling one and militates against an easy moral view of history. Sometimes, the prophets of the Old Testament seemed to make clear distinctions between the good and bad nations; theirs was a simple formula of "this nation will fall because it is evil; that nation will endure if it repents and becomes good." In history, as in personal experience, it must be admitted that relatively innocent nations suffer the ravages of war. Belgium and Finland, in the last war, are perhaps cases in point. We are not saying, of course, that these two nations were Simon pure, that they achieved the moral law, but compared to Germany, Italy, Japan, and Russia, they were relatively good, yet they were caught between the titans and suffered. This fact is a warning to moralists who suppose that all suffering is a punishment for immorality. Christianity would say no. This is an example of the suffering of the innocent which we do not really understand. To be sure, Christianity goes on to say that even this type of suffering is not ultimately tragic.

Suffering may be an avenue to new and creative heights. There are many examples of both nations and individuals who, because of their suffering, have achieved noble creations. Therefore, pain is not an unmitigated evil *per se*. In our bodies pain is uncomfortable, but it is a warning that we must have something fixed. It is, therefore, a help to improve us. Suffering on the larger scale may also be a means to improvement and maturity. And if the life of Jesus is also a clue, it is clear that suffering is part of life, and may be a means to a very creative life. Nevertheless, this should not be expanded into the dogma that *all* suffering of *all* kinds is essentially good. Most types of suffering *may* be, but not all kinds are beneficial. When Victor Hugo said that "poverty in youth is the nutrition of character," he committed this fallacy. Poverty in youth *may* be conducive to strong character, but it also may result in the destruction of character. Thus, Christianity would say that various kinds of suffering in life are inevitable; it is a part of life. Why life wasn't built some other way, we do not know. Given, then, the presence of suffering, what can we do? We believe that most suffering can be turned into a creative use. On the other hand, there are some kinds of suffering caused by nature or men which are horrible and destructive. These experiences baffle us; these tax our faith. Why some men know such suffering, and others not, we do not know. Our only healthy response is to renew our efforts to eliminate situations which give rise to these agonizing horrors. It is quite understandable why a man who is in the midst of one of these tortures cannot believe in God. On the other hand, there are many examples of people who have suffered greatly and who have also retained, even increased, their belief in God. This, too, is a mystery.

B. *Historical Interpretation*

The other problem in interpreting history is the scientific problem. The secular historian quite rightly questions the validity of the Christian view of history. He asks to what degree our theory can be derived from the facts and events; can it be validated by empirical data? He is rightly suspicious that our view is a *theory,* not a scientific conclusion, and, therefore, it is just another theory, no more reliable or helpful than any other theory. Christianity would agree with most of these criticisms. We admit that our "interpretation" means going beyond dates and places. It means, by definition, giving a pattern to events. Thus, we agree at the start that our view is an interpretation, not an empirical formula.

We would also want to say, however, that *all* views of history are interpretations, that there can be no pure, scientific view of history. A purely scientific history would be nothing but a chronicle of events listed chronologically, and it would have to include *all* events no matter how large or small. For to leave out anything would be to omit a fact, and to make a value judgment about "insignificance" or "unimportance." As soon as we ask questions about the meaning of events, we are beyond mere recording of data and are at once involved in a mixture of fact and interpretation. The scientific historian, of course, can give us more than naked facts; he can also tell us about causes and effects, and relationships between various events, but he cannot always assert that one event was solely caused by another event. There may be many minor contributing causes, such as intangible, psychological forces. In addition, the scientific historian cannot, in terms of his scientific method, give us meaning, value judgments, patterns, and purposes to historical events. This role is the domain of the philosophers and theologians. In the last analysis, therefore, the problem of theories of histories is not so much whether we will have an interpretation or no interpretation of history, but rather *which one* will make the most sense to us; which one will we adopt. And again, in the last analysis, this involves a choice between faiths. The Christian view is derived from its faith, from its experiences and interpretations of God, Christ, the prophets, and revelation. If these primary presuppositions are not accepted, it is difficult to accept the Christian view of history. If these doctrines are accepted, then the Christian view does, we believe, make sense.

However, we should add a word of caution. The Christian interpretation of history, like most other views, is essentially a general one. Indeed, part of our view is the assertion that history is paradoxical, complex, orderly, yet spontaneous. For this reason we can offer no accurate detailed explanations or predictions. Whenever people have claimed specific accuracy on detailed events, they have erred—in Christian theory or in Marxian theory, or in some other view. This points up both the limits of all theories and the limits of all human insight. Christian theology, no less than any other philosophy of history, cannot lay claim to exact historical interpretation or prediction. We must work hand in hand with the scientific historian. But we do believe we have enough evidence for our general over-all interpretation. On any specific application of our view, we must be ready to change our application if the facts so warrant it.

C. *The End of History*

The final part of the historical problem concerns the end of history. And here again, obviously, we are faced with an essential mystery. Because we are creatures of time and space, it is difficult for us to imagine what the end of time means, or what it is like. This is why the New Testament is filled with myths, symbols, and allegories, when it discusses this problem. The Bible suggests that the end of history means the final battle between good and evil in which evil is defeated and the triumph of good completed. This means that the Kingdom of God, the establishment of God's sovereignty, is then fulfilled. Time, in the historical process as we know it, is over, and eternal life is realized. Questions such as *when* this will occur and where in the universe the "kingdom" is established, we do not know, nor can we even imagine in terms of a date or some planet. All ideas about the end of history and eternal life are derived from our experiences and the teachings of Christ, the events of the Cross and the Resurrection, and our interpretations. The

Doctrine of "The Last Things" (eschatology) is a logical conclusion of these other data, but the conclusion is necessarily
hazy, vague and general. The truth is we know extremely
little, and there is no way in which we can learn much more.
It will remain another one of those mysterious adventures of
the future. The problem is important primarily as a logical
consideration of the implications of the Christian view of
history. Some statement about eternal life, the Kingdom of
God, and of history, and judgment is necessary if the problem of good and evil is to be met. It will not do intellec-
tually, in Christianity, to say that there is a problem of good
and evil in history, and proceed no further. We are duty
bound to say what we believe about this problem. Hence,
theologians have talked about the Last Judgment. And
although we have mentioned some of the crude descriptions,
they are at least an attempt to state that evil does not finally
triumph. The Doctrine of the End of History is an attempt to
say what we believe will happen and why. In general, we
believe the New Testament gives us the answers—eternal
life with God—but we must remain exceedingly humble
about details. For even the New Testament and apparently
Jesus, or His disciples and biographers, were wrong in their
details, as for example, the prediction that the Kingdom
will be fulfilled "in this generation." By the same token, we
should not take the highly symbolic language as literally
true, nor even a particular allegory, such as the final battle of
Gog and Magog, and "the fire of Heaven" which consumed
Satan (Revelation 19), is adequate. Such descriptions point
to a truth beyond, part of which may be captured in a symbol, part of which may be portrayed by someone in a new
symbol, but none of which shall be known until the End.

The sum and substance of the Christian interpretation of
history, regardless of our ignorance of much of the process,

is our firm belief that history is not a meaningless chaos, nor a tragic force, nor a blind machine running nowhere. It is the Christian faith that the process of history is moral, that it has a purpose, that God is its Lord, that it is therefore essentially meaningful and worth-while, and that its final culmination is the Kingdom of God in which we shall all be "fully known even as we are now known" in fellowship with God.

DOCTRINE OF SALVATION

WE COME now to the final doctrine, that concerning salvation. This also involves the process called conversion. Salvation means a saving *from* something and conversion means a turning *towards* something. The two words together, therefore, indicate a negative and positive process; not only a turning away, but also an advance towards something new and creative.

The first concern, then, is the problem of salvation. *From* what is Christianity trying to rescue us? In old-fashioned language, it is the power of sin which holds man from salvation. If we recall what was said about sin and anxiety in the chapter on the nature of man, it will perhaps help us to see the relevancy of the Doctrine of Salvation. By way of summary, we described the tensions of man, how man is a bundle of tensions, how man does not like insecurity and anxiety, and therefore seeks to escape. Man always believes he can solve his anxieties successfully, one way or another. Thus, anxiety is one of the conditions which lead to sin. Christianity, we said, believes that man, by his own efforts, cannot escape or solve his insecurities. But man always thinks he can—and this is his sin. This kind of pride, therefore, is also the essence of sin. We gave further definitions of sin when we described man's response to tensions as indicative of an attitude of self-sufficiency. Man believes he is wise enough, strong enough, and good enough to master his problems. Therefore, he has no real need of God. In this sense, sin is also disobedience of God. Then we went on to give various examples of man's attempted escapes or solutions to anxiety and why, from the Christian viewpoint, they were inadequate if not finally destructive.

The problem, therefore, as Christianity sees it, is how can man live with his tensions, curb the conditions which produce sin, and break the power of sin? In a word, how can man be saved from himself? Again, Christianity insists that man cannot save himself—only God can save man. The Doctrine of Salvation and Conversion, Christians believe, is the description of how God saves man.

A. *The Conversion Process*

The method of conversion here outlined is somewhat artificial. For the sake of clarity, specific steps are described, but in an actual conversion a person may not follow these steps in this order; some of them may be reversed. And in most cases, the basic elements are not as distinct and separate as they are in our description. Indeed, stages usually overlap, now come into the consciousness, now fade away, then return again mixed with other influences. Thus, what we are wary of is pretending that there are seven easy steps to conversion. There is no easy way in this process because it involves a fundamental change in personality, and it affects our total personality. Salvation and conversion in Christianity are not getting rid of a few bad habits, or tinkering around with a few "noble thoughts," or doing a few good deeds per week. It is always a long and gradual process that requires some inner wrestling, and results only in gradual reformation of a person.

Mindful, then, of the limits of our method of description,

what are the fundamental aspects of conversion? First, one must become aware of his tensions and anxiety. We have said that Christianity sees all men as basically anxious. The fact is, however, that not all people are aware of their anxiety; it may still rest deep in their unconscious. The problem for this type of person is how to bring his anxiety into his conscious experience. There is no one method for this. It may occur in a number of ways. Certain types of experience, such as a narrow escape from death, or the problem of old age, or the meaninglessness of a job, might raise the problem to his consciousness. Or, most people are aware of anxieties but misinterpret them. They may feel that if only they got more income, or if only the right girl came along, then all anxieties would disappear. So the primary step is either to become aware of our anxieties, or to re-interpret correctly the anxieties we already have. This is not to say that all anxieties are the same or of equal importance. We distinguished the three major kinds of anxiety as spiritual, neurotic, and guilt. What is important here is to become aware of one or two samples of each kind, and particularly the clues to spiritual anxiety. As we shall see later, Christianity makes no claim to solving deep-seated guilt anxiety problems. This is the domain of the professional psychiatrist. Our primary concern is with spiritual restlessness. Therefore, a person must have some awareness of his spiritual anxiety if he is to take steps towards curing it.

The second major step is that of becoming aware of the futility of escapes. This means that the anxious person has tried various escapes or answers for his insecurity, and found them wanting. Various flings at "fads," social causes, and "new thought" movements, may have been tried and found unsuccessful. This type of person is dissatisfied, often frustrated, with every answer he has tried. They do not work. He knows it. He is aware of the uselessness of trying to escape his tensions. And this leads immediately to the third step.

In the third step a kind of despair about both anxiety and the attempts to escape it seem to be involved in the conversion process. The use of the word "despair" here is dangerous perhaps. What is meant is the feeling of "giving up," of ceasing to struggle. A person must have the attitude of realizing the futility of trying to escape by one's own effort. Despair here means that one is still very much concerned and bothered by his anxiety, yet he is also discarding *his own* attempts to eliminate it. Despair does *not* mean here the attitude of utter hopelessness about one's whole life. Quite the contrary; one gives up his struggle, yet he still retains the deep desire for self-acceptance and integrity. This is the healthy, though difficult, attitude of despair. However, we do not all achieve this attitude. Thus, in this critical period— and it often is very critical—some people do go through a very dismal and morose period. Real despair—hopelessness— is the lot of these people. On the other hand, different types of people do not experience any profound sadness at all. For them this period may be either neutral or mildly pleasant. And, of course, there are all shades of degrees in between these extremes. William James, in his famous book, *The Varieties of Religious Experience,*[1] has some excellent descriptions of these varying responses in this conversion period. At any rate, regardless of the degree, there does seem to be a strong element of despair—a giving up the struggle to escape, yet yearning for integrity and meaning to life.

The fourth step is that of humility and repentance. These are the old-fashioned Biblical words. Humility does not mean being "a mouse"! Christian humility is not self-abnegation, the pretense of acting like a nobody, and being a door mat for other people to walk on. It is not the Uriah Heep

[1] Longmans, Green, New York, 1922. See especially Chaps. 4 through 7.

humility of cringing, fawning, and agreeing with everyone. Quite the contrary; Christian humility means the rigorous acceptance of one's self *as he is.* It is the recognition of one's real condition of character—the good, bad and indifferent. This is why Christian humility is a very difficult virtue. Most of us think more highly of ourselves than we ought to think, though a few of us think too lowly of ourselves. Humility is self-acceptance *as we really are.* Repentance is almost the same. It means casting aside the *false* views of self. Repentance has often been associated with the word "sorry." Christian repentance does not mean feeling sorry for oneself, nor does it mean feeling sad for one's mistakes. It means primarily the giving up of pride of outlook, pride of self, and the acceptance of the true picture of one's self. Thus, repentance is the act of giving up pride, and humility is the attitude of self-acceptance.

In the conversion process, this fourth stage of humility and repentance means the acceptance of one's real condition of anxiety, of inability to solve it or live with it, and the dislike or dissatisfaction of remaining as one is. This is somewhat paradoxical but, I believe, true. This stage means real self-acceptance with all the anxieties, and yet at the same time, there is a healthy sense of dissatisfaction, a desire for meaning and creativity. This is a creative anxiety for it prevents us from smugness and vapid self-contentment. On the other hand, it is not a desperate self-hatred which seeks to vent itself dramatically. Rather, it is a quiet but steady longing for self-fulfillment. This is why humility is so central in the New Testament. It is and can be an enormously fruitful stage in personality growth and in the conversion process.

Again, following immediately, is the fifth step—that of the desire to get well. This attitude was implied in humility, but in order to distinguish it from healthy self-acceptance, we use the phrase "desire to get well." By this we mean a definite desire for meaning in life. In Biblical terms, this is the "thirst after righteousness," the search for "grace," the seeking for "the abundant life." The desire to get well, therefore, means a deep desire for creative living, loving, and self-completion. In psychological terms, this meaning might be akin to "the will-to-live," though we mean more than survival; we mean the achievement of a higher kind of existence. Moreover, this profound yearning corresponds to the image of God in all men. In a sense, therefore, the desire to get well may be the image of God operating in one's personality. This is what Augustine meant when he said that grace prompts us to ask for more grace.

This may seem to be laboring the obvious. But we stress the point because some people do not want to get well. This is literally true with a few people—they really are tired of life and want to die. But a larger number of people do not want to get well in the sense of changing their lives. Also, we emphasize this point to indicate that conversion is a voluntary process. One cannot be exhorted, urged, or commanded to grow. A person must *want* to grow. A man cannot be cured psychologically against his will nor can he be converted religiously against his will. This is also why personal decision has an important place in religion. Whatever else "decision" may mean, the key element here is the voluntary and personal responsibility the individual plays in the process. Christianity indeed goes so far on this point as to say that not only is it impossible for a minister to force conversion upon a person, but even God cannot (or will not) save a man against his will. Thus, even if all the other conditions of conversion are met, this inward and personal desire for salvation is essential.

Before proceeding further, let us summarize the five steps: (1) Recognition of dependent, anxious, and sinful condition; (2) Awareness of inability to escape or live creatively in this condition; (3) Abandoning attempts to solve the problems by one's own efforts; (4) The acceptance of this dilemma as the real situation; and (5) The deep desire to achieve self-fulfillment and meaning. These stages are necessary for conversion because they mean that a person has faced reality. If these five steps are fulfilled, it means that a man has already lost much of his inordinate egotism, his anxious self-interest, and his frantic pretenses. In a very exact sense, he has both faced and accepted the truth about himself and about the nature of personality structure. In addition, he has also the healthy attitude which seeks new growth, creativity, and adventure. He has at least a spark of faith in reality—a spark which seeks to become a flame.

The next step involves the question of where does one get more faith, more help? If we are speaking of the Christian faith, then obviously, one must become acquainted with Christianity. Familiarity with the Christian faith is this next stage. This can occur through obvious contacts with the Bible, the Church, books, and people. Acquaintances with these media are necessary if one is to obtain some knowledge about the Christian religion. And it should be stressed that this is not merely intellectual knowledge about doctrines or statements, though some of this is important, but is primarily a search for interpretations of one's religious experiences. This is a way which may provide an answer for what one feels or hopes.

It is the Christian faith that if one is in the situation of meaninglessness and humility, and if one is made familiar with the Christian story, this story will appeal to him and make sense. To be sure, it may be only vague at first, but it will be meaningful enough for him to trust it, and then proceed to work out the details as he goes along. Indeed, this has been the experience of Christians throughout history. Some acquaintance, then, with the Christian description of

God, Christ, history, the nature of life, faith, and values, is essential if one is to know anything about the object of his search.

The next step is "the leap of faith." And this is the most difficult for moderns to understand. It is quite natural for us to demand proof before we commit ourselves to anything. We are all aware of the dangers of a blind faith, of uncritical allegiance to any movement. It is healthy for us to ask questions about other people's promises, to want to know for sure how something works out. But there is a wide gap between blind faith and naked fact. Neither a bare fact nor an unknown faith is of much use to anyone. Our real choice, not only in matters of religion but in all areas of life, is usually a mixture of certainty and mystery, of something provable and of something not easily proved. The process of conversion at this point is precisely this compound of certainty and mystery. This certainty is usually a set of ethical and religious experiences which are recognized as such by the individual. In addition, he is quite sure that his other experiences in life have given him some clue as to the nature of reality and himself. He is certain of his anxiety, his limitation, his dependency, and his yearning for meaning. He may even have had some vague awareness of God, either through the New Testament picture of Christ, or through other people, or his own beginnings in prayer and ethical action. The net effect of one or all of these experiences is that the individual regards them as significant. He trusts these experiences in the sense that he is very sure they are enormously important. He seldom understands their full import, nor is he able to state precisely a pattern of detail and logical order. But he is certain that they are profoundly meaningful and offer unlimited possibilities for further exploration. In short, "something" has begun to happen to a person; he knows it, likes it, finds meaning in it, and wants to search further. This set of experiences, then, is his base of certainty.

The "leap" of faith is necessary because no individual is ever certain beforehand that he will find God, or if he finds Him, whether he will want to continue the relationship. One must also face the possibility that particular doctrines in Christianity may not be meaningful to a person. One set of descriptions may not correspond to the individual's experience. Therefore, he may not feel at home in any particular theological "school," or denominational Church. There is no way that one can prove beforehand that Mr. Jones will be an Episcopalian, or that Miss Smith will end up a liberal in theology. Or, the Trinitarian Formula may be very meaningful to one person, while someone else finds it a definite barrier and prefers some other description or symbol. Thus, there is no one particular guarantee where a person will find his spiritual home. On the other hand, the leap is not a blind jump. It is safe to say that while one does not know *which* formula or Church he will accept, one does know that he will join *some* Church or theological view, or perhaps start a new one which combines the traditional features of many systems or denominations.

Our primary concern here, however, is to say that Christianity cannot prove by either scientific demonstration or philosophical argument that God can be found through Christ, through the Church, and through people. Nor can Christianity guarantee that all men will find God this way or that way. An individual person can have no absolute proof that he will find the object of his search. This is why we use the term "leap." For it means that a person has to go beyond immediate data, experience, and argument. It means that he launches out on a new adventure, the outcome of which he does not know. He can hope, he can be optimistic, but he cannot know absolutely. Faith in this sense is a launching out on a new adventure; it is a leap beyond what one has already experienced.

At the same time, Christianity says this is not a blind faith. We defined blind faith as believing something that isn't so— like $2+2=5$, or that all Negroes have a different kind of blood. But in Christianity, the leap of faith is not blind because one is not closing his eyes to anything; on the contrary, he is opening his eyes wider. He is not overlooking facts or discarding knowledge and experience; he is trying to enlarge and expand his understanding. Furthermore, his adventure is not blind because he has before him the testimony and experience of thousands of other Christians. At every step one can compare his experiences and interpretations with those of other Christians throughout history. In addition, one cannot say this leap is blind because Christianity hopes that the individual will continue to test his new adventures with his old ones. This means that we do not dispense with our intellect and other previous knowledge, and then seek God in dumb and uncritical awe. It is assumed that if one is to mature in the Christian faith, he must analyze and evaluate his progress every step of the way. One must strike a balance between reason, experience, and faith. This leap of faith is a jump to a higher level of insight and meaning, and, if valid, should result in new understanding and appreciation of all areas of life. So Christianity sees this kind of a leap of faith as indispensable to the conversion process.

From another point of view, it is difficult to see why this leap of faith should be so troublesome for moderns. What we have described above is not so different from many other human experiences. The leap of faith is really not at all unusual, nor confined to religious experience. For example, there is no proof that Mr. A. will be a success in his chosen career; there is no guarantee that Mr. B. will live to the ripe old age of eighty-five. No young couple can ever prove beforehand that their marriage will be a lasting and happy one. Yet the fact remains that most people launch out on a career, plan to live many years, and get married. One could raise exactly the same kind of cynical questions about these "adventures of faith" that is done so often against religion. Pessimists have charged marriage as an adventure in blind faith; cynics sometimes say we are stupid to plan for tomorrow. But the vast majority of us can answer these superficial barbs, and we answer them just the way Christianity does. Our reply is that we admit that we are not absolutely certain of success, old age, and happy marriage. But we also emphatically deny that these adventures are blind. Why? Because we have enough knowledge about ourselves—our abilities, training, capacities, and maturity, to *trust* that we have a good fighting chance. We trust what we do know will guide us through what we do not know. Furthermore, others have gone before us; we can learn from them. Our faith, therefore, is based on empirical data, sound analysis and reasoning, and it also goes beyond, not in spite of, *but because of* the known evidence.

So we come back to one of our earlier statements about faith. Nearly all the most important adventures and decisions in life are made by faith. We get an education, start a career, plan for the future, and get married, without any absolute certainty that these things will work out. We have a lot of evidence to go on, but never conclusive proof. This is why we literally "live by faith," not by guarantees. The adventure of finding God requires this kind of faith. This faith is not something esoteric and magical; it is fundamentally the same as is found in all other human adventures.

Up to this point in the conversion process it is especially significant to note that all the steps here outlined are almost exactly the same as the process of integration in psychiatric treatment. It is perhaps no accident that psychiatry now seems to have arrived at a process that exactly coincides with the Christian process of conversion. With a few changes in labels our seven steps of conversion could be equated with the seven steps of psychiatric integration. For example, a patient must meet the following conditions: (1) He must first be aware of his neurosis (anxiety); (2) He must be aware of the futility of escaping his neurosis; (3) He must give up trying to solve his neurosis by his own efforts; (4) He must accept his real condition, neurosis and all. This means he must have some self-acceptance and integrity. (5) He must have a desire to get well, want to be cured; (6) He must have some acquaintance with the enterprise and principles of psychiatry, some trust that it is a valid and helpful viewpoint; (7) He must make a leap of faith—that is to say, he must seek out a doctor in whom he will place his life.

But which doctor? There are so many doctors (ministers) around, what is best? Faced with this question, the intelligent patient inquires about professional (Church) requirements, training, and ratings, in order that he may find a qualified doctor. In addition, perhaps the patient asks other people. One way or another, he finds out that a given doctor has helped other people. But there is no guarantee that the doctor can cure *him*. Yet on the basis of evidence he goes to a doctor, and trusts and hopes that the doctor can help him. In so doing, he surrenders and puts his life into the care of the doctor. In precisely the same way, Christianity speaks of Christ as the doctor, or as Luke said, "the beloved physician."

Our point in this long comparison is again to emphasize that conversion is not a deep, dark mystery that is unrelated to human experience. We are trying to say that the conversion process is a very human one, that, indeed, it is a natural one in the sense that it is available to everyone; that it coincides with so many of our other life experiences. We stress this because some people have tried at times to make conversion either too simple or too magical and complex. Sometimes, we have over-rated the dramatic exceptions, such as Paul on the Damascus Road, or Augustine in the Bishop's garden. Even in this type of experience, we have overlooked the long and gradual experiences which preceded the dramatic climax, and the long wrestling and struggles which followed. In all cases of conversion, it is clear that there is no *one*, isolated, and sudden experience. The total process is long and gradual. Some few individuals may have a dramatic or ecstatic experience *in* addition to the other experiences. Most of us do not. It is dangerous, therefore, to believe that we do not know God unless we have some clear-cut vision, all at once. To expect only this kind of experience will probably produce a bogus hallucination and close our eyes to genuine experiences of God.

On the other hand, conversion is not as simple as raising one's right hand and saying, "I believe in Jesus Christ." This act *might* be *one* step, but by itself it is not the whole process. One's character is not changed by raising the right (or left) hand. Conversion is, therefore, a long and gradual process, but also a very normal one and a very human one. It is an adventure, not a pilgrimage of fear, nor an escape from reality, but *the* venture of life.

The next problem we must seek to answer is what does conversion do to a person, what difference does it make? We have arrived at the point where we have said that a man must take a leap of faith, must launch out on the adventure of finding God. Thus, the first question is, "Faith in what?" And obviously, Christianity answers by, "Faith in God." But what does this mean in terms of a person himself? Is is the Christian affirmation that if we adjust ourselves to the ultimate reality and nature of things, we will be able to live a more creative life. This is the belief that what is the most real and lasting will help solve our less real and changing problems. Most of us, semi-consciously at least, have some awareness of this ultimate reality or most real. That is to say, most of us believe and assume that there is "a power greater than ourselves" operating in the universe. We believe that this power makes for some order in nature and history, that there does seem to be some purpose and law of life as a whole. In short, we are all aware of a "something."

But faith in a "something" is not enough. A "something" is really equal to a "nothing" in terms of effect on our personality. And this we know already, so we seek to know more about this "something," this reality. We want to know something concrete if we are to display faith. Therefore, Christianity suggests that if we want to know more about God, we should look at Christ because God was present in Christ. As was noted in the chapters on Revelation and Incarnation, this has been the historic Christian statement about how one knows God. Christianity recognizes the universal human experience of being aware of a power greater than ourselves, of feeling that there is an ultimate reality, a purpose, an order to life, a "something" that is the ground of all existence. But in addition to these experiences of God, Christianity believes that the prophets offered further clues to the nature of God, and that finally God revealed Himself most clearly and fully in or through Jesus Christ. Thus, the faith of the Christian is not just faith in a something, but faith in the God we know in Christ. This means that a person can have a real personal experience of God. And, of course, this is the testimony of thousands of Christians throughout history. This is the empirical story; namely, that when confronted with the Christ of the New Testament, the Christ of the Church, and the Christ in the hearts of Christian people, thousands of persons have felt acquainted with God. And this new relationship has produced a new transformation of character. On this basis, Christianity affirms its conviction that this is the *best* and most complete way to know God. It does not mean that other religions and philosophies know nothing about God; it means that we believe *this* is the way anyone can obtain *more complete* knowledge of God. And, of course, the final reminder is that *no one* can know *all* about God.

Let us now analyze as specifically as we can what this kind of faith does to a person, what difference the conversion process makes. One major result is security. We have said that the basic problem of man is anxiety. If conversion or salvation is to be of any real value, it must meet this problem of anxiety. Christianity believes that faith in God answers the situation. How? Trust in God means that one has organized his life upon a basis, a reality which does not change but remains constant and lasting. Though we do not know in detail all about the nature and activity of this Reality, or God, we know and experience at least its essential sameness and permanence. Thus, there need be no anxiety about the real source of one's power and foundation. By contrast, if one's God, one's "determiner of destiny," is a person, a nation, a social movement, or a picture of success, these gods may be destroyed or collapse at any time. Inordinate trust in an economic or political system is always accompanied by the fear that the system may collapse; such anxiety produces a sense of insecurity, and inspires frantic actions to avoid the threat of disaster. This does not make for a stable personality. On the other hand, if one's ultimate loyalty is to *the* God, there is no worry about the God dying or failing. Hence, the basic anxiety is removed.

This idea can be translated into other terms. Faith in God produces the feeling of "being at home in the universe," or the attitude that "life is worth living." A living relationship with God means that one has found a basic meaning in life, which is not just a subjective description of an isolated experience, but the feeling that, however expressed, one is in league with the very structure of life itself. Whatever it is "that makes the world go around," one experiences this power through his own life. These are some of the more homely phrases that mean the same thing, that is, adjustment to reality. When this adjustment occurs, then the spiritual anxiety about whether life has meaning, whether it makes sense, whether *my* life is worth-while, is solved. A relationship with God gives man meaning, makes life worth-while, and therefore removes this basic anxiety. This is the inner peace that the New Testament speaks of, the inner security which the world can neither give nor take away. From the Christian viewpoint, this is *the one* basic and essential security. This is the rock foundation upon which the house of one's personality is built. Without this basic security, all other securities will be inadequate. To continue the New Testament parable, no matter how ornate or even how solid the other parts of the structure are, they will not long endure unless the foundation is secure. The basic security, therefore, in the Christian faith is religious certainty—the experience of feeling at home in life—a living relationship with God.

At the same time, we hasten to point out that this basic security is radically different from smugness or self-contentment. There is nothing in the Christian faith which promises man external security; that is, protection from all the vicissitudes and problems of life. In fact, the New Testament says, in effect, that if we take Christianity seriously, we will probably have more problems and difficulties than if we avoided Christianity. If we take our religion seriously, it means that our conscience will be made more sensitive; it means that we will assume responsibilities we otherwise would neglect, and it means that we will seek to do more good works than we otherwise would do. Also, once committed to our faith, we will be required thereby to take a stand on moral issues when others can afford to be silent. Our point is that Christianity offers no easy solution or promise of an undisturbed, isolated life of irresponsibility.

There is nothing in the Christian faith which says that faith in God will result in economic, political, social success, and security. There is nothing in the New Testament which says that a true Christian will be spared pain, worry, and trouble. In other words, most of the tensions of life remain. We will always have to struggle and fight with external problems. In addition, we will always have to wrestle with our inner tensions and problems. This is the way of life itself. This is why Christianity brands as false all men or religions which promise man complete peace and freedom from worry. "Living without tension" is a false promise; if achievable, it would be a stagnating death. Guarantees of success and easy prosperity if only "one has faith enough" is not the Christian faith. "Peace of mind" or "soul," if it means no internal problems or external concerns, is the sleep of death and the height of irresponsibility. Salvation does not mean offering us an easy irresponsible escape from this world, but rather, providing us with power and meaning to live *in* this world. This is why Christianity can never be an escapist religion. Its primary concern is to enable us to live creatively in this life; if this is done then we have begun already to experience eternal life. Christianity, therefore, does not claim to solve all our anxieties. It claims to help us solve our basic religious anxiety.

B. *Justification by Faith*

Since Christianity claims to answer religious anxiety and yet insists that other anxieties remain with us, we must face up to the problem of whether Christianity can offer anything in the face of those other anxieties. The Christian answer here is that we do not believe it is possible to live without tensions and anxieties, but we believe Christianity gives us the power to *live with* these tensions. The situation of daily life, as Christianity sees it, is something like this. We are all faced with numerous daily decisions, most of them fundamentally moral. How shall I vote on this or that measure? What should be my reaction to my neighbor in this and that situation? How should I treat my child when he does thus and so? As a Christian, one tries to decide these questions on the basis of love and justice. At the same time, the Christian knows that he can never be sure his decision is right. On social issues, we are never sure we have all the facts available; we are never certain how a measure will work out in the long run. In our personal relationships, the sensitive Christian is always aware of the conflict between self-interest and love of neighbor. We know we do not love "with all our heart and soul and mind." In short, all ethical decisions in life are imperfect; they fall short of the ideal. In addition, therefore, to the tensions and anxieties involved in making the decisions, we know that, judged by absolute standards, we are guilty of imperfection. This realization of guilt produces, in turn, more tension. The Christian ethic claims to hold up the perfect standard of perfect love and justice. At the same time, the Christian religion tells us that none of us is perfect and never can be. We are therefore faced with the dilemma of knowing in advance that no matter how much we do, we must fall short and are therefore guilty. This could be an intolerable and destructive situation if it were to end as described. But Christianity tries to meet this problem by its Doctrine of Justification by Faith.

This doctrine has often been ignored and forgotten in Christian history, but it remains a central one in the New Testament and especially in Protestantism at its best. What is the essence of this doctrine? The purpose is to enable man to hold on to a perfect standard (so as not to get lost in relativism) and to live creatively in a situation of anxiety and guilt. Let us see how Justification by Faith proposes to do this.

We have said that the key relationship in Christianity is that between man and God, and that this "fellowship" is one of faith. That means an active commitment to the God we know in Christ. We also stressed the point that Jesus used the symbol of "Father" when speaking of God. This symbol is particularly meaningful in this Doctrine of Justification by Faith. For the relationship here between man and reality is much like that between father and child. And the doctrine can best be explained in terms of the human father and child. From a parent's point of view, the child always falls far short of the standards of adults. In a very real sense, the parents have a perfect ideal but are faced with a youngster who, by definition, cannot now achieve the ideal. The problem for both parents and child is how to establish a relationship that will be creative rather than destructive, yet without discarding the norms of adult maturity. If the father should continually condemn the child for being immature, if he only judges the child by pointing out his daily failings, he will create a terrible anxiety and sense of guilt in the child. Soon the child will be afraid to do anything for fear of making a mistake and "catching hell." Soon, too, the child will retreat within himself, build up his own defenses against his father, construct a dream world of phantasy and he is well on the way to neurosis. Or, should the father never criticize his child, but condone everything he did, the child would soon become an insufferable egotist and probably an unrestrained tyrant or bully.

There is another alternative, however. If the father should gently but firmly point out the mistakes and creatively criticize, indicating as well his loving acceptance of the *child as he is,* then a new relationship is established. That is to say, in this method the father does not condemn a six-year-old for failing to act like a twenty-six-year-old adult. He does judge the child in terms of what a six-year-old should do. In short, he expects the child to act like a six-year-old. This standard is held up to the child. Praise is given when he meets the standard, gentle criticism when he does not. Now, if the child knows that when he is "doing his best" and it turns out badly, his father will forgive him, then life is tolerable. For forgiveness means that his father accepts him as a person and, therefore, the child can accept himself as a person of integrity and worth.

Forgiveness does not mean ignoring the broken window, the minor theft; it means that the father understands why the child did those things, that these are part of the normal six-year-old behavior capacity. The father will tenderly explain why these things must be soon outgrown. And if the child acknowledges the deeds and sees the point and the motive of his father's "talk," the chances are he will soon outgrow these actions. But this all depends not so much upon the specific talk, but the whole relationship between parent and son. The essence of this is, of course, love. But in this context, the son has *faith* in the love and justice of his father. He *trusts* that his father will not beat and berate him. He *believes* that his father will understand, forgive, and accept him. The child, therefore, is justified by his faith. Or, to put it another way, if the child does live up to the norm of a six-year-old, then his father *"accounts him as righteous."* Naturally, the six-year-old is not as righteous or mature as a twenty-six-year-old, but if he is living up to his fullest capabilities, he is accounted as righteous as a twenty-six-year-old. The twenty-six-year-old elder brother who lives up to his full ability is, therefore, no more virtuous in the eyes of his father than the six-year-old who is also living to the full extent. Both are equally "good" even though their specific actions differ radically. Both are dependent for their maturity and virtue on their faith relationship with their father. Because they have this type of trust and because their father responds to them this way, they are relieved of guilt; they are justified by this faith. The fear of punishment, of pure negative condemnation, the anxiety of wondering if "I will be found out," is gone and with it the guilt of being "caught." Thus, the destructive attitudes of anxiety and guilt are eliminated. At the same time, there is no easy tolerance of everything they do. Rather, there is a real motivation for improvement and growth. Love and faith combined with justice provide creative power.

This is precisely what Justification by Faith involves in Christianity. The love and faith relationship between man and God works exactly the same way as the human relationship. The Christian knows that God does not consign us to hell for this or that imperfection. If, like the child, we are humble and repentant (as we defined these words), then God is quick to forgive. We carry on in our daily ethical decisions knowing in advance that we fall short but also knowing that, if we are aware of this fact and are seeking to improve, we need not be anxious or guilty. But this attitude is dependent upon our faith, our active trust in an active God. We are justified, therefore, by our faith.

C. *Sanctification by the Holy Spirit*

The last part of the salvation-conversion process is the Doctrine of Sanctification by the Holy Spirit. This concerns not so much intellectual growth as it does the experience of power. We have indicated that conversion means the expanding of one's insight and understanding of life, a broadening of one's intellectual horizon. But religion is not merely an intellectual process. Since we are dealing with the total personality, salvation must involve the heart and soul, too. We have also tried to show how conversion affects man's anxiety and helps to solve his basic insecurity. The other aspect of salvation is the experience of renewing power. Since God is the power of love, among other things, an experience of God results in the new power operating through a person. In our Doctrine of Man, we stated that one other basic problem of man is his lack of love for other people, and his self-love or egotism. The problem, therefore, is how man can get new power to love other people. Christianity believes that this capacity comes from a relationship with God. This is why the New Testament says that love of God comes before love of man. If a man loves God, *then* he will be able to love men. A continuing relationship with God means that undue self-love has broken down. The center of one's existence and concern is no longer the self, but God and man. This means that our vitalities and drives are channeled outward, and, therefore, our interests and drives are channeled outside the self. This makes for creative personalities and creative actions. On the other hand, if all our energies and drives are turned inward, only on ourselves, then we become like a covered pot which boils; that is, all steamed up inside with no outlets. But if we have a funnel, some method which provides creative outlets, then all the "steam" is directed, and is powerful and useful.

The conversion process affords, therefore, not only useful outlets for our energies, but provides the method for it. Augustine made the daring statement, "Love God and do as you please," and what he meant by this was that a person who has a living relationship with God loves to do what God pleases. A person loves to express God's love in his daily life.

He is thereby freed from compulsions and frustrations, his personality has new power, new spontaneity, and new fulfillment. An experience of God, therefore, really means the experiencing of the power to love. This is probably the one clear test of salvation: the power to love. If a man does not love people, he probably has not experienced God however loudly he may proclaim his devotion. In fact, Jesus made this point crystal clear when He said that whoever does not love his brother or his neighbor does not love God. We may say, then, that the essence of salvation in Christianity is the power to love, that this power is not naturally present in man as he is, but that it is obtained by a living relationship to God. God is love and an experience of God means that this love operates in and through man. This is the "difference" that Christianity can make in a man. This we believe is man's deepest yearning and need. All of us, above all, want to love and to be loved. Christianity believes that this is precisely what God does for man. God loves man and gives him the power to love. Salvation is a rescue from a loveless life.

If we are correct in defining salvation this way, then it should be apparent why conversion is not a quick once-and-for-all affair. The power to love is not something that is achieved overnight. It is a long and gradual growth. And because love is dynamic and spontaneous, there is no static level of perfection. We shall never reach the position when we can say, "Now I love perfectly; there is nothing else for me to do or to know." If that were possible, it would mean the death of love, for then we would become smug and would stagnate. The glory of love, human and divine, is that it never stops growing. No matter how much we love, we find that we can learn to love more. It is a life-long adventure in which we never have to worry whether we will exhaust its joys and pleasures. This is why we cannot say that we know all there is to know about love, and why we cannot say we are completely saved.

There is another reason for the endless process of salvation, too. The "Old Man" is always with us! Experiences of God do not wholly destroy our basic attitudes and personality structure. No matter how realistic and creative is our relationship with God and people, we all have our "dry periods," our "ups and downs." As in human relationships, regardless of how high a character, there are periods of strain, of "lukewarmness," and of inner protest. This is normal. For these reasons, we have to be refreshed, re-invigorated, and re-oriented regularly. This is why prayer, study, meditation, and worship in church, are so essential. These practices fortify us, "keep us on the beam," strengthen us. To assume that we do not need to "practice" our religion this way is the height of pride. Such an assumption rests on the idea that we are good enough, wise enough, and loving enough to live life on our own. This type of person is very hard to live with—in or outside the Church. By the same token, anyone who assumes that he is completely saved, that he has no further need for the Church, is, according to the New Testament, the worst of sinners. For this is the cardinal sin of spiritual pride. The fact is that we are not perfect and never will be perfect. This fact alone should guard us against assuming that conversion is a once-and-for-all affair.

Conversion, then, is a life-long process, and our job is to keep it growing and enlarging. In short, man still has internal conflicts and anxieties and problems. We are not saved *from* these; but we are saved *in order to* battle them successfully. Salvation is a harmony of conflicts on a new level. The old level of basic anxiety about the meaning of life is gone. The new level is on the firm basis of meaning and inner security, but there are problems here, too. We shall always have conflict between one desire and another, one will and another. Anxiety in the form of concern about people's welfare and moral justice will and ought to be present. This is a creative type of anxiety for it is seeking improvement rather than desperate clinging to an image of the past, or fear of losing something in the present. But our point is that all the daily problems will still be with us. Salvation does not mean that our economic problems are solved, our financial burden lifted, the neighbor's barking dog silenced for our comfort. The external problems and arrangements of life are the same. It is the inner person who is changed by conversion. The Christian claim is that an internally reformed person can meet his external problems with more poise and power, and, in the long run, become more a master of events rather than a victim of circumstance.

Sanctification means, therefore, a process of becoming better, not merely morally, but spiritually as well. This means that Christianity's ideal is to remake the whole man better in *all* departments—the abundant life. Sanctification by the Holy Spirit means that this process is best furthered and maintained by the God-Man relationship as it is experienced in the Church. We defined one view of the Holy Spirit as a special way in which God acts through the Church. Historically and psychologically, it is clear that many people find God through a "community of believers." Very few find a continual and growing relationship with God in isolation. This is why Christianity believes that the Church is the *best* (not the only) way to grow spiritually. In this sense, sanctification by the Holy Spirit means common religious growth together in the Church.

In the broader sense, sanctification by the Holy Spirit means any individual's continuing experience of God whether in the Church or in one's private devotional life, intimate friendships, and ethical actions. It is unfortunate that in the past there have been debates between the narrow and broad definitions of the Holy Spirit. Among theologians, some of this is necessary in the interests of precision and logic. But in terms of conversion and sanctification, it is difficult to see how any theologian can dogmatically assert that God can work through this particular channel or church, and not through some other channel or church. It would appear more appropriate to acknowledge, with the New Testament, that God works in "mysterious and diverse ways" and is not bound by the narrow confines of ecclesiastical pride.

What is important about the Doctrine of Sanctification by the Holy Spirit is that it is the keystone of the conversion process. This doctrine is not really concerned about the problem of finding God within or without the Church; it is primarily concerned with stating how necessary it is that all Christians experience a continuity of power, a continual and growing relationship with God. Or we might put it this way: Justification by faith is the establishment of a faith and love relationship between man and God, and sanctification by the Holy Spirit is the positive growth of that relationship.

We may summarize this chapter on salvation by emphasizing again these main points. Conversion is a process; it is not a sudden, single experience, nor is it achieved by magic or theological formulae. Conversion is a life-long adventure involving the total personality. The factors in this "reformation of character" are essentially natural and orderly in the sense that experiences of God are not unrelated to everyday human experiences. The final aspects of the total process, such as justification by faith and sanctification by the Holy Spirit are open to all and can be shared by all. For each individual person who is just beginning on this greatest adventure in life, there is the problem of the leap of faith, the sense of mystery. Yet all "beginners" have the record and experiences of millions of Christians who have gone before and the New Testament witness of what God wrought in the human clay of the disciples and apostles. And we know that our faith and labor is not in vain, so "thanks be to God who giveth us this victory through our Lord Jesus Christ." This is victory which gives understanding instead of confusion, faith instead of anxiety, and love in place of fear.

FINIS

Appendix

APPENDIX A

SOME CONTEMPORARY VIEWS ON THE DOCTRINE OF CHRIST

ONE of the reasons many moderns do not believe in the classical (orthodox) Doctrine of Christ is probably the use of ancient theological language, which does not seem to fit in with modern knowledge. Hence, when the Creeds and Church theology describe the Divinity of Christ as the God-Man idea, "very God of very God," many tend to dismiss such terms and say, how could a man be both God and Man at the same time? Yet it is surprising how many people believe Jesus to be something special. Many protest quite vigorously that they hold to no "divinity of Jesus" dogma, but do believe that He was "the best man that ever lived," and that the world would be a far better place if all followed His teachings. Indeed, many contemporaries are quite ready to accept Jesus as a kind of model or pattern for creative living. Some people will refer to Jesus as "Master" or even "Lord," but still will not tolerate the Divinity idea or the Incarnation doctrine.

So today, both within Christianity and outside of the Church, there are thousands of people who regard Jesus as the supreme example for living yet who will brook no theory of Divinity or God-Man idea. Moreover, most of these people would call themselves "liberal" in their outlook and regard themselves as outside of the "conservative" or orthodox school of theology. Indeed, some orthodox Christians have tried to declare that these "liberals" are not Christians at all, that if one does not agree to the Doctrine of the Incarnation and God-Man, one cannot be a Christian. This kind of attack has confirmed the liberal suspicion that the Doctrine of the Divinity of Christ is old-fashioned, narrow, and ridiculous. And by way of reply, the liberal has usually insisted that he is still just as much of a Christian as his conservative brethren and perhaps more so because the liberal has an open mind and does not accept dogma placidly or uncritically. So even in our present time, there is still a controversy over the problem of Christ. Much of this controversy, as in the past, is unnecessary.

It is the opinion of this writer that the liberal and conservative are much nearer together than they think, that their differences stem largely from a too literal interpretation of their respective descriptions of Christ, and from a too hasty judgment of what the other really *means* by his statements. For example, when a person says that he does not believe Jesus to be divine, but that he believes Jesus to be the best man that ever lived and worthy of following, what is he saying? He has said and done several things. First, he has made a value judgment about Jesus. In saying Jesus is "the best man," he has some criterion or standard of value by which he has rated Jesus and other great men, and rated Jesus first. But what is this standard? How does one decide what is "best?" Best from what point of view? Jesus is best as teacher, idealist, liver of life, etc.? But these terms do not really tell us much; for the issue is: How does one decide what kind of teacher, idealist, liver of life, is best? When one says "best," he must have some idea or conviction or faith of what is "best." Yet most liberals never think this value judgment through, they do not define or explain what their standard is, what "best" is. Second, when the liberal states that Jesus is worthy of emulation, one could ask the same question of why Jesus is worth following. And the answer would be the same as above: because He is best. But what is best? And so the circle is completed.

But more important, one could raise the question of whether it is wise for people to follow any *one* man. Is any man, however noble and good, worthy of being called "Master," worthy of being followed as closely as we are able? Is this not dangerously close to the dictatorship principle, idolatry of a man? If one is urged to follow only the teachings of Jesus, there is the danger that, like the teachings of any great man, some are good, but some are not so good. And who decides what are the good and the bad ones? From what point of view? Or, if one is urged to follow the person of Christ, there is the danger of slavish imitation which tends to destroy our own individual personalities. These are some of the logical difficulties of the liberal statements about Christ. But the fact remains that most thinking liberals are fully aware of these dangers and they are the first to say that these pitfalls are not what *they mean* when they make their statements. And the conservative critic often overlooks what liberals are trying to say.

Very well, what are the liberals trying to say? They are trying to avoid the pitfalls of the historical controversies about the nature of Christ. They do not want to get caught in the difficult position of having to defend the idea that if Christ was the God-Man, does He thereby have two natures —one human, one divine? And how could such a dual nature be possible? The liberal position, therefore, tries to avoid such obtuse arguments and to replace them by a more simple and effective explanation. Further, the liberal is trying to say that the life and teachings of Jesus are extraordinary and of inestimable value for mankind, and that, therefore, Jesus is worth following as a man, and that His teachings should be put into practice because they will work for the benefit of all. And where does God come into this, a conservative might ask? To which the liberal would reply, "God is in this all the way." That is to say, God worked through Jesus just as He works through all people. The wisdom of God is seen in all great men, prophets of all religions—Jesus, Socrates, and Buddha. Jesus has given us additional insight into the nature of life and how it may best be lived. And is this not enough? Is this not reasonable and understandable? Why should this simple truth be cluttered up with a lot of mumbo-jumbo and dialectic dogma? If the writer understands the main sentiment, such is the liberal position.

What can be said concerning this view? Sympathy and appreciation of this position have been stated, and its validity as against the conservative attack has been implied. But one or two comments should be made. First, this writer would say that what the liberal really *means* by his statement is not very far from what the conservative really *means* by his position. As far as the author can see, the liberal's practical relationship to Jesus is the same as that of the conservative. For the liberal in practice is devoted to Jesus, lives by His teachings, and tries to develop attitudes similar to those exhibited by Jesus. Thus, in a very real and practical sense, Jesus is the master of life for the liberal. At the same time, the practical relationship of the conservative is nearly identical. For the conservative, also, is devoted to Christ, tries to practice His teachings, and cultivate the inner attitudes of Christ. Here, too, Jesus is Master and Lord. Where the two differ is in their *theoretical* explanations of Christ. The liberal may tend to give a humanist description, the orthodox a divine explanation. Both are aware of the difficulties and pitfalls in the *other's* description, but both tend to overlook or minimize the difficulties in their own definition. And, of course, there are many types of liberal views and many types of orthodox views.

In general, each school is the same, but they will vary in detail. Thus, there is always the argument as to whether one should say, "God *was* in Christ" or "God *worked through* Christ," or "Jesus was the Perfect Man but not Divine" or "I'm a humanist but I agree Jesus was the best man that ever lived." Now, for all practical purposes, this writer cannot really see much essential difference. For example, what is the difference between perfect and divine? Or, if all is merely human, then how does one say "best"—"best" according to what standard? Or, what is the precise difference between God working (acting) through Christ, and being *in* Christ? So far as the author can see, there is no essential or radical difference. And the more the writer sees active Christians who hold these slightly different theoretical definitions, the more convinced he is that in practice the result is the same, that in action, Jesus *means* the same and does the same for all.

Practically speaking, some liberals believe in the divinity of Christ but theoretically do not. That is to say, in following Jesus and trying to live as He did and by His teachings, they are accepting Him as a kind of God. For them, Jesus is their determiner of destiny, the guide or authority which shapes their lives. If Jesus is the "best," He is also the Highest, the most worthy to be emulated. And as noted earlier, God is generally defined as that which gives meaning to life, that to which one gives his loyalty or devotion, or that by which a man lives. Thus, when the liberal says he follows Jesus as best, or worthy, and believes the world should be guided by His teachings, he has, in practical effect, made Jesus divine. That is why the author would say that the modern liberal position believes in the practical divinity of Christ, but many liberals do not believe in the theoretical divinity of Christ, and if one had to choose between one position or the other, this writer would choose the liberal position. For we would all be far better off if people were practicing the divinity of Christ instead of believing in the theory of it without practicing it. Of course, the ideal is to hold to both and achieve harmony of thought and action.

The final comment on the liberal position is the criticism that in their attempt to avoid the difficulties of theoretical arguments, some liberals have not dug deeply into the weakness of their own theoretical groundwork. As was suggested earlier, the statements of Jesus as "best" does not solve some of the problems of knowledge. The liberal has not faced the difficulties of how one can make value judgments, what criteria are necessarily involved, and how one arrives at such standards. The liberal has *assumed* some set of values, some view of life, and has made judgments accordingly, but he has not examined how he arrived at such assumptions and whether they are valid or not, and whether they can be proved as valid, or are part of one's faith. This is the whole problem of epistemology (knowledge) and faith, and this is one of man's most complex and difficult problems. There are no simple answers or "self-evident truths" here. And should the liberal begin digging here, he would find himself in the company of the orthodox theologians who, at best, are at least trying to harmonize these theoretical problems with practical actions. Perhaps it is no accident that liberalism was strongest in America in a period when Americans displayed tremendous practical activity and tended to ignore theoretical problems.

The conservative or orthodox position should now be examined. It was said that this view is derived from the New Testament account of Jesus as being in some way the Incarnation or Revelation of God. The problem for the Church theologians was to explain and try to make this experience of the disciples intelligible and defensible to others, as well as to themselves. The problem was complicated by attacks from two sides. One attack (the Gnostics) tried to make Jesus out as wholly divine and to discard His humanity altogether. Another attack (in several forms—Arianism, Apollinarians, etc.) tried to discard the divine aspect and emphasize only the human. Thus, when one reads Christian theology as it defended itself against the Gnostics, it looks as though Christianity was over-emphasizing the human side, and when the Church was defending itself against Arianism, it appeared that Christianity was over-stressing the divine side. But a careful reading of each of the Church's statements in the light of the total Doctrine of Christ, will reveal that Christianity was trying to maintain both aspects. Thus, the orthodox view is in the extremely difficult position of dealing with a miracle. This is the only honest and frank word to use here.

There is no use pretending that the belief in Jesus as the God-Man is a simple rational idea, or that it can be proved by a direct appeal to pure, historical evidences. This is why the problem of evidences and the problem of knowledge was stressed early in the book. This is why it was emphasized that the decision about Christ is one that goes beyond scientific data, and inevitably is decided upon the basis of whatever evidence there is, interpreted by personal faith and from within Christianity. That God should invade time, space, and history at a particular period in the person of Jesus of Nazareth, is not an everyday occurrence; that people should, in terms of their experience and interpretations, come to believe that in some special way God was present in—incarnate in—Jesus, is not open to simple explanations. It is, therefore, unusual, extraordinary, miraculous, and there is no wisdom in trying to pass this off as something quite simple and obvious. Faced, then, with this mysterious yet overpowering event, theology is bound to explain it as best it can.

But any good theologian knows his own limitations and the limits of theology itself. This humble wisdom of the

Church theologians resulted in several creeds, many "systems," and many controversies. Had there been no such humble insight, there would have been one creed, one system, and no arguments. For truth would have been captured, defined, explained and believed with no further debate. To be sure, there were less humble churchmen who assumed they had arrived at the total story, and who tried to enforce this assumption. But they were always challenged and were never completely successful. Protests and Reformations arose—and they always will and should if Christianity is to grow. Thus, in the history of Christian thought, there are several descriptions of the nature of Christ, but what seems to be common to all of them is the firm conviction that God was in Christ in a more complete and special way than in any other person in history.

As to just *how* God was in Christ, in *what* precise *way*, who can say with exact authority? This is why there will always be debate on questions such as these. If God was in Christ, does it mean that Jesus was without sin? What part of Jesus was man—His body? What part was God—His spirit? What about the biological problem of two natures—what about free will and foreknowledge? What about Jesus' mistakes in prophecy, Virgin Birth? These and a host of similar questions are the result of honest minds trying to track down the full implications of the God-Man idea. As can be seen, these are enormously difficult questions filled with mystery. Most of them are so difficult and complex that they can probably never be answered or proved beyond a shadow of a doubt. The lazy mind will stop and wave all the questions aside and say that they are a waste of time. But to a rigorously searching mind, questions must always be examined and ordered, and thought must balance with action.

So in theology, the search goes on. What is important is that each answer, or set of answers, be asserted with reservations and humility. This has not always been the case, and people have been read out of Christianity because of disagreement over one of these secondary problems. This is the great danger of the orthodox position. In trying to preserve the faith, the conservative often tends to regard ancient creeds and statements as sacred and true just because they are the tradition. He tends to accept too literally early formulations, and to forget that these statements were designed to meet special problems of culture at a special time in history. The Church's answer to Arianism in the fourth century may not be the right answer to the mechanist of the nineteenth century. The conservative also tends to forget that the "saints" who helped make tradition were, nevertheless, human beings and that the "saints" were saints partly because they were the first to admit their limitations.

The conservative is much at fault for his hasty condemnation of modern liberalism. Part of this orthodox error is the facile judgment that because liberalism uses different language and symbols it must mean something radically different. This assumption is not necessarily true. As suggested above, what many liberals mean is the same as what conservatives really mean—at least in terms of living. That they are often apart in thought is probably true. And here both are to blame, for the liberal tends to ignore theoretical problems and the conservative tends to over-emphasize them. The author cannot pretend to settle the dispute here nor be so foolish as to present *the* system upon which all can agree. There are differences; there will be; there ought to be, on many things. But the writer is suggesting here that in addition to the differences, indeed, at the source of the variances, lies a profound and common agreement—Christ.

The final answer, therefore, as to the nature of Christ and how one comes to decide upon it, is no different than that recorded in the New Testament. We contemporaries, liberal, orthodox, or somewhere in between, in the last analysis have very little to add to the New Testament. For we have there the account of men who, in experiencing Christ, were convinced that they were experiencing God in a most real and complete way. This evidence is there for all to examine. But whether any of us today also become personally convinced that God was in Christ will depend upon our own decision when we are confronted with Christ and with all the other evidences that are available.

It should be clear now that one cannot be argued into this belief, nor can it be proved beyond all doubt either by rational demonstration or scientific proof. The real decision, which is common to thousands of Christians throughout history, is based on the confrontation of Christ, by which a person comes to believe intensely that he is also experiencing God. That is why the Christian, in one way or another, will describe these experiences as finding God in or through Christ. What actually happens in most cases is something like this: A person seeking some meaning to his life becomes aware of various general ideas about God. These he receives from his education and the culture in which he lives. He also has various experiences in life which lead him to formulate religious or philosophical interpretations about the order of nature, what human beings are like, and perhaps that there seems to be or must be some kind of basic reality or power behind all of life. From certain religions, he may accept some descriptions of this reality, such as purposive, moral, or all-pervading. And all this will vary with individuals.

But if the person also becomes acquainted with Christ and the Christian story, new possibilities are available. He may come to learn a great deal about the Christian faith, share in its fellowship (the Church), and then flatly reject the whole business. He may conclude that Jesus was just another man and not a particularly great one at that, and that the whole

Christian religion is preposterous. This does not happen very often, but it does happen. We in the Church would like to think that in such cases the person was merely uninformed or ignorant of the real Christian faith, and that, if only the person really knew the depth and power and rationale of Christianity, he would not reject it. But the fact remains that some few people do know a great deal about Christianity and still reject it. The reasons for such rejections do not lie in ignorance, but deep in the experiences, personalities and motivations of the persons involved. It would be very difficult for any outsider to fathom out "the why" of a rejection. The proper course of action for Christians would seem to be to refrain from any disparaging judgment and to treat such persons with a healthy and friendly respect.

To be sure, there are many other persons who abandon Christianity, but the majority in this case do so largely because they had a bad taste of it in Sunday School. Most people today who reject Christianity are in reality rejecting a childish view of religion, or some particular narrow view of it. And in this case, the reasons usually are unpleasant experiences with corruptions of Christianity, in addition to ignorance of the true Christian faith. But the point here is that there is no all-compelling magic about the personality of Christ or the activity of God. The point is that when confronted with Christ, there is no automatic conversion. The New Testament makes this very clear. For while Jesus' life and agony on the Cross impressed many people, it is also true that Jesus made no impression whatsoever on other people. The most dramatic example of this is the New Testament picture of the Crucifixion. Some of the followers and relatives of Jesus were there and were in great sorrow. Other people were there also, who probably felt that here was a noble man horribly crucified, and that perhaps God was here and was about to do something to redress the wrong. But also there were some soldiers who, at the foot of the Cross, were having a crap game. What supreme and bored indifference! So it should be clear that the experience of Christ does not compel us against our will to experience God or become religious.

At the same time, it is equally true that millions of people have come to know God through Christ. Most of these may have followed the same approach as those who rejected Christianity; that is, they have sought meaning, and had general ideas about God and life in general. But as they came to know Christ, they came to know more about God and life. God was no longer a principle or vague idea or some kind of power, but God now seemed to be real, more personal. Life seemed to be less of a puzzle, more meaningful. God seemed to be more a part of one's life, rather than confined to the area of speculative ideas. Thus, for those people the description of Christ as the God-Man seemed to be most accurate. For in terms of their experiences, it is quite true that they came to know God through or in Christ. This, then, is the central starting point of Christianity—that God reveals Himself to mankind in and through Jesus of Nazareth. This central affirmation is derived from the experience of the disciples and apostles, and has been continually corroborated by Christians ever since. All other statements, arguments, and doctrines are derived from this common point and are attempts to describe, explain, and fit it in with the rest of life.

Before ending this Appendix some mention should be made of derived explanations and arguments. Again, it must be emphasized that these descriptions do not prove that God was in Christ, but they do tend to make it at least credible and understandable. The Doctrine of the Incarnation is a dogma that has been described already. The formal statement of this tenet is that God incarnated Himself in the person of

Jesus of Nazareth, that while God partially revealed Himself or was disclosed by other prophets and religious men in the past, in this instance He acted in a special and more complete way. Hence, the Incarnation is also called Special Revelation. This means that God revealed Himself most fully and most completely in this special way—in Jesus of Nazareth. That this seemed to be anticipated by the Old Testament prophets lends credibility to the event and later description.

The idea of the Incarnation was defended in a series of arguments put forth first by St. Paul. Paul raises some negative questions. He asks, in effect, "Suppose Jesus were not the Christ; suppose he was just another fine man?" And Paul replies by pointing out that if Jesus were just another man, then we are rather badly off. For it would mean that Jesus' ideas and teachings about God were just some more human guesses and opinions. And there is no reason why we should accept Jesus' opinions instead of those expressed by other religious figures. Therefore, we would still be in the dark about God and the meaning of life. If Jesus were only a man, it would be slavish and immoral to deify Him and follow Him as Master, for no man is wise enough and good enough to be Lord over all other men.

Further, says Paul, if Jesus was a great man and He was killed, what does this tell us about the character of life? There are many great men in history and most of them were killed for their convictions or actions, as Jesus was. Does this not suggest, therefore, that the Good is crucified in life? Does this not seem to indicate that evil wins out in life, that good does not succeed? If Jesus was a great man, or even if He were divine, the fact is He was defeated and killed. Would this not confirm the notion that good men, and good plans, do not succeed? Paul suggests that it would. And if this is so, then he says, "We are of all men most miserable" (I

Corinthians 15:19). Paul's solution here, of course, involves the Resurrection.

Paul uses the resurrection story as an argument indicating that the Good (Christ) was not finally defeated, but was finally triumphant because Christ was raised up, thereby overcoming death and evil. Nevertheless, Paul's two questions are important: First, he asked, if Jesus was just another great man, on what ground and by what standards should we follow Him rather than somebody else? Secondly, if He— whether divine or human—was defeated and killed and there was no Resurrection, does this not tell us that life is essentially evil, meaningless, and tragic, and make fools out of all of us, including God? The implied answer to Paul's question is that only if Jesus were the Incarnation of God, and only if He were in some way resurrected, could we believe in Him. Mankind should accept the authority of God as absolute and no other. Therefore, if Jesus be not God, we should not accept either Him or His teachings as authoritative for our lives. Since Paul and the rest of Christianity believe in the God in Christ, Jesus is accepted as authoritative.

From this conviction follows the definitions of Christ as Savior, Redeemer, the "Light and the Life and the Way." These terms have often led to confusion because when they are overemphasized, it seems to make Jesus a separate God, and the charge of dualism is often made. But these labels are used to express the idea that through Christ, God acted and made Himself known, that it was through Christ that we come to know the power and wisdom of God. We are, therefore, saved through Christ. Christianity never meant to say that there was a God somewhere who remained aloof, and that Jesus was another more concrete God who really did the work. All that is meant by these labels is that God's power and wisdom is best known through Christ, more clearly seen and experienced in this way. Again, such terms are part of the Doctrine of the Incarnation and are merely symbols which, in the New Testament period, meant the activity of God. If Jesus were in no sense divine—if He were entirely a man and no more—then the terms Savior and Redeemer would be erroneous. For again, Christianity would insist that no man, however great, could ever be the savior of all men or the redeemer of them. And modern history, as well as ancient, would seem to confirm this conviction. Because of the self-styled saviors of history, such as Hitler and Stalin, we know from bitter experience that no mortal can ever be our savior. Any mortal who claims he is our savior will destroy us if we give in to him. This is why Jesus steadfastly resisted invitations to become the immediate political savior of Israel, why He insisted that we are saved not by men but by the power of God. So, Jesus is our savior only in the sense that God was acting in and through Jesus—for it is the *God* in Christ that is the Redeemer.

These are the main secondary arguments about the nature of Christ. There are tertiary ones and more. All the complex and detailed debates and problems about which part of Jesus could be called human, which part divine, cannot be dealt with in this book To do so would involve an historical recount of many technical and scholastic arguments. None of them prove or disprove the central Christian affirmation that God was in Christ. They are important for theologians to wrestle with, and they must be re-examined constantly by the experts, whose job is to try and fit in all the problems into some intelligible pattern. For laymen it is important to wrestle with such problems if intellect or experience demands it. The assumption here is that most of us have other primary problems to settle first. For those who are so advanced, there are advanced books on the subjects, well-written and thoroughly scholarly in treatment (see Bibliography).

APPENDIX B

A PROBLEM CONCERNED WITH "WHO KILLED JESUS?"

THE issue of anti-Semitism in the New Testament has been raised in contemporary literature. This problem is also connected with the question: "Who killed Jesus?" There have been some attempts to show that the Jews had nothing to do with the death of Jesus, that it was the Romans who were really responsible for the Crucifixion, and that some of the Gospel accounts reflect anti-Semitism.[1] Further, that modern Christians should still believe that the Jews crucified Jesus, it is suggested, shows the modern Christian's unconscious, if not conscious, hatred of the Jews. In fact, some authors have labelled the Biblical account as a gigantic hoax. In answer to this charge, it should be pointed out that the best and virtually all Biblical scholars have quite thoroughly shown this charge to be false. We cannot recount here all the historical and textual evidence, indeed volumes, in support of the general accuracy of the Biblical account. The scholarship is available to any who wish to read it. We can, however, summarize the answer.

First of all, in these times of great stress and racial bias, the recent terrible destruction of six million Jews by the Nazis makes it very understandable why we should want to combat all types and sources of anti-Semitism wherever it appears. This applies to Christianity as well. There is no

[1] Pierre Van Passen, *Why Jesus Died;* Dial, New York, 1949.

doubt that there are some remarks critical of the Jews in the New Testament. But it is very doubtful whether it is anti-Semitism in the modern sense. It is enormously significant that such remarks are not made on the basis of race, but on the basis either of behavior or of religious and ethical opinions. Furthermore, criticism did not include *all* Jews, but certain schools of Jewish thought. This is normal, and part of it, at least, healthy. If criticism alone is to be regarded as "anti-Semitic," when the Jews are the subject of the criticism, then the Old Testament prophets were the most virulent offenders. No passage in the New Testament can match the vigorous criticisms of an Amos or a Jeremiah. And, like the Old Testament, some of the New Testament critics were themselves Jews. There were arguments, for example, in the Jerusalem Church as to whether the mission of the Church was to the Gentiles, to the Jews, or to both. This was a strong argument which aroused bitterness and disunity. Yet there is no evidence that the controversy was a racial one. The New Testament cannot be accused of anti-Semitism on the grounds that some Jews are put in an "unfavorable light" or are "harshly criticized." If this is the basis for the charge of anti-Semitism, then it means that either all Jews should never be criticized, or that they are all gods who are above criticism. No responsible Jew, or any other person, would ever make that claim. It would also mean that the New Testament is anti-everybody since Jew and Greek, barbarian and Gentile —all human beings—come in for some severe criticism at one place or another.

Having said this about the New Testament, we must also readily acknowledge that in later Church history and to the present day, there have been individuals who have displayed anti-Semitism. Here we deplore the fact, and categorically state that insofar as any Christian is anti-Semitic, anti-Negro, or against any particular race he betrays his faith and acts contrary to the New Testament. The ethic of Jesus that we are all children of God and that love one to another becomes us, is clear enough refutation. Because some people try to corrupt a principle does not make that principle untrue.

Next, we must turn to the question of who killed Jesus. The Biblical record states that *both* the Jews and the Romans were responsible for the death of Jesus. The general view is that certain of the Jewish leaders, for several reasons, saw Jesus as a threat either to the established religion, or to the complex and precarious political relations between Jewry and Rome. Accordingly, these groups of Jewish authorities wanted Jesus out of the way. Under Roman occupation, however, the Jews had no authority to take a man's life. If Jesus were to be executed, only the Romans could do this. It was necessary for the Jewish leaders, therefore, to convince Rome that it was advisable to do just that. This move was successful. Thus, both Jew and Roman had a part in the Crucifixion of Jesus. Such is the bare outline of the situation.

The story is filled with tremendous complexities, most of which are recorded in the Biblical accounts. The whole tragic drama is a confusion of different motives, plans, hopes, sudden reversals, changes of tactics and strategy, unexpected new developments, and changing public opinion. If the Gospel record seems confusing, the reader should remember that the situation itself was exceedingly confusing. To imagine that the death of Jesus and all the circumstances which led up to it, was a simple affair, easily described, is pure fancy. Yet some modern critics seem to think that the circumstances were very simple, and the New Testament writers botched up the whole business in the interests of anti-Semitism! Again, the full weight of the scholarly evidence supports the accuracy of the Gospel accounts. To be sure, the accounts do not answer all the questions and there are some discrepancies, but there is also a remarkable degree of accuracy and agreement. What is abundantly clear on this point, is that neither the Jews nor Romans were blameless in the death of Jesus. It is simply not true that one or the other was *solely* responsible. It is quite clear that *both* were responsible. Only the scholars can figure out the degree of percentage.

To close this part on anti-Semitism, Christian theology would make two very strong and forthright statements: First, whether certain Jews did or did not contribute to the cause of Jesus' death is a minor fact compared to the vast number of Christians who have crucified Christ in their hearts. All Christians betray and corrupt in part the spirit of Christ. When we fail to love our neighbor, we betray Jesus; when we give in to cheap envy, vicious hatred, and petty prejudices, we are spiritually crucifying Christ anew. Since we ostensibly accept Christ as our Master, our guilt is far more serious than those Jews who did not see Jesus as Lord. Thus, Christian theology would cast severe judgment not upon men like Caiaphas, but upon Christians.

Second, whatever part these Jewish leaders played, it illustrates a profound and tragic truth; namely, the harm that good people may do. The Sanhedrin authorities and certain chief Pharisees were not devils. By and large, they were good men, long schooled in their religion, educated, intelligent, sincere in their religious convictions and loyal to the interests of the Jews. From their point of view, Jesus was dangerous religiously because His prophetic criticisms threatened the established religion, and because His claim of divine authority seemed blasphemous. Secondly, Jesus seemed to be dangerous politically in that certain nationalistic groups might have tried to capitalize on the public ferment and possibly have used or tried to use Jesus as a "front." Jesus' claims to the Messiah (if made) were probably interpreted politically by most people. At any rate, given the convictions of Judaism at this period, it is quite understandable why these leaders should reject Jesus and regard Him as dangerous. So, here was a tragic situation in which sincere and relatively good men crucified the Good in the name of the Good. And again, Christianity would put no special guilt on these Jews, but would again point out the lesson here. The "good" people in any society often make equally tragic mistakes. The more power one has, the more terrible his mistake may be. Thus, a general in the army has the power to order thousands of men, but his decision, if wrong, may cost the lives of many thousands. Such a man is no special form of devil; he is no more evil than the rest of us who make only small decisions. The point is that a good and able man in a place of power is often caught in a terribly tragic situation.

So much for arguments and explanations. The main points again are that anti-Semitism in the modern sense is not present in the New Testament, that Christian theology specifically repudiates it, and that our debt to the Jews and their religion is immeasurable. This is why Pope Pius XII could say that "spiritually we are all Semites."

BIBLIOGRAPHY

Aulén, Gustaf: *Christus Victor*. New York, Macmillan, 1931. The shortest and most clear review of the various interpretations of the Doctrine of the Atonement.

———— *The Faith of the Christian Church*. Philadelphia, Muhlenberg Press, 1948. One of the best recent treatments of Christian dogma. Not easy reading, but very complete.

Baillie, D. M.: *God was in Christ*. New York, Scribners, 1948. One of the best, if not *the* best book on the nature of Christ, Incarnation and Atonement. Very readable.

Baillie, John: *Invitation to Pilgrimage*. New York, Scribners, 1942. A disarming and inspirational account of one modern from scepticism to faith.

Barry, F. R.: *The Relevance of the Church*. New York, Scribners, 1935. The significance of the Church; an interpretation from a liberal Anglican position.

Brown, W. A.: *Christian Theology in Outline*. Constructive, readable description of Christian theology from a sound liberal viewpoint.

Butterfield, Herbert: *Christianity and History*. New York, Scribners, 1950. One of the most recent and best books on the Christian view of history. Very readable.

Casserley, J. V. L.: *No Faith of My Own*. New York, Longmans, 1950. A concise statement of the Christian faith written primarily for those who are not convinced.

Fitch, Robert E.: *The Kingdom Without End*. New York, Scribners, 1950. A brief, clear and delightful book on God acting in history. Timely and relevant.

Forsythe, P. T.: *The Church and the Sacraments*. London, Independent Press, 1949. The significance and meaning of the Church; an interpretation by an English Congregationalist.

Grant, Frederick C.: *An Introduction to New Testament Thought*. New York, Abingdon-Cokesbury Press, 1950. The best summary of the theology of the New Testament. Scholarly but well worth the effort.

Hazen Books on Religion, The. Distributed by Association Press, New York, 1937. Although very elementary and brief, these books are an excellent starting point for anyone beginning his first venture into the Christian faith.

1. Bowie, Walter R.: *The Bible*
2. Calhoun, Robert L.: *What is Man?*

239

3. Harkness, Georgia: *Religious Living*
4. Horton, Walter M.:   *God*
5. Lyman, Mary E.:   *Jesus*
6. Stewart, George: *The Church*

Hodgson, Leonard: *The Doctrine of the Trinity.*   New York, Scribners, 1944. A modern restatement of the Trinitarian Formula vis-a-vis contemporary philosophy.

Kirk, Kenneth E.:   Ed., *The Apostolic Ministry.*   New York, Morehouse-Gorham, 1946. An Anglo-Catholic interpretation of the Church.

Lewis, C. S.:   *Beyond Personality. The Case for Christianity. Christian Behavior.*   New York, Macmillan. These three short books provide an excellent introduction to some of the basic Christian beliefs. They are distinguished by their remarkable clarity, simplicity, and wit.

Manson, T. W.:   *The Church's Ministry.*   Philadelphia, Westminster Press, 1948. A reply to *The Apostolic Ministry* from Protestant evangelical position.

Niebuhr, Reinhold.   *The Nature and Destiny of Man.*   New York, Scribners, 1948. Not easy reading for the layman, but more than worth the try even if only to know what is causing people to praise and damn "that man Neibuhr!"

Pittenger, W. Norman: *The Historic Faith and a Changing World.*   New York, Oxford University Press, 1950. Well written and clear presentation of the Christian faith with special attention to its relevance to American culture.

Quick, Oliver C.:   *Doctrines of the Creed.*   New York, Scribners, 1941. A careful and balanced discussion of the theology behind the historic creeds and their meaning in the life of a Christian.

Richardson, Alan: *Christian Apologetics.*   New York, Harpers, 1947. One of the best attempts to provide empirical support to the Christian faith while retaining the classical Christian view.

———— *The Gospel and Modern Thought.*   A compact treatment of the relation of the Gospel to present day issues in thought.

Vidler, Alec R.:   *Christian Belief.*   New York, Scribners, 1950. A short and concise but profound statement of Christianity as stated in the Creeds.

Whale, John S.:   *Christian Doctrine.*   New York, Macmillan, 1948. Clear explanations of the basic Christian doctrines such as God, Man, Sin, Christ, Salvation, etc.

INDEX

Date Due

APR 27			
May 11			
FEB 6			
DEC 17			
NOV 21			
DEC 5			
Demco 293-5			